Scripture in Context Series

▲

Church Doctrine & the Bible

T0350071

Scripture in Context Series

Church Doctrine & the Bible

▼

Theology in Ancient Context

David Instone-Brewer

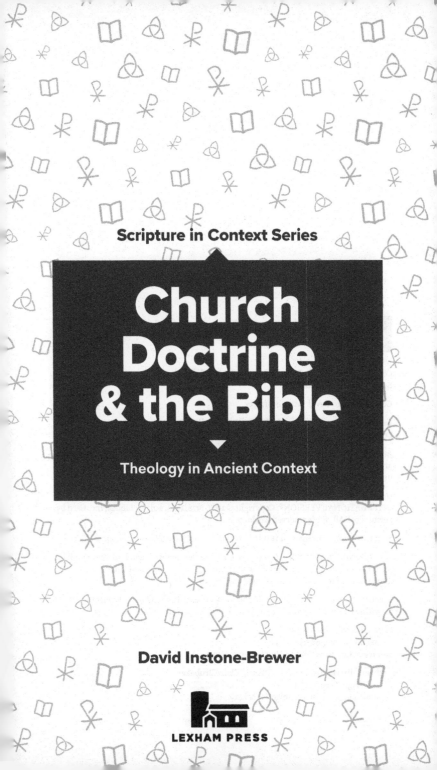

LEXHAM PRESS

Church Doctrine and the Bible: Theology in Ancient Context
Scripture in Context Series

Lexham Press, 1313 Commercial St., Bellingham, WA 98225
LexhamPress.com

Print ISBN 978-1-68-359376-8
Digital ISBN 978-1-68-359377-5
Library of Congress Control Number 2020931312

Lexham Editorial Team: Elliot Ritzema, Claire Brubaker
Cover Design: Owen Craft
Typesetting: Justin Marr, Abigail Stocker

Contents

Section 3:
Doctrines That Matter

▼

Introduction

Doctrines are the church's conclusions about theology in the Bible. But would its first readers agree with modern doctrines? This book digs into the Bible text to discover whether the original readers would have drawn the same conclusions. This method ends up revitalizing some doctrines and invites revision of others. It even suggests we should reject a few.

Let me begin this book with a confession: I normally work in biblical studies, which means I don't usually delve much into theology or church doctrine. This might sound strange, but like every academic discipline, biblical studies and theology are becoming more specialized as knowledge grows. (After all, an expert is someone who knows increasingly more about increasingly less!) The separation between theology and biblical studies has become problematic, because theologians are sometimes tempted to ignore the Bible, and biblical scholars feel that theology isn't always grounded in the text. For example, when Wayne Grudem planned to base his *Systematic Theology* on the Bible, some of his fellow theologians derided the idea and tried to dissuade him. Fortunately, he ignored them.

The difference between theology and biblical studies is similar to that between theoretical and practical physics. The practical physicists at the European Organization for Nuclear Research break up atoms to discover the building blocks of matter. The theoretical physicists at the same institution try to build a theory to explain all the particles that have been discovered. But what if they found a theory so beautiful and simple that they decided to ignore any further discoveries? They might decide that the atom is made up of protons, neutrons, and electrons, and that this "trinity" is too perfect to tinker with. The discovery of other particles such as the Higgs boson would then be a "heresy," and creating something like a quantum computer would be ruled out as impossible before anyone got started.

Similar silliness can happen in theology if we forget that it should be built on data found in the Bible and not just on theories that work well for a time. The true test of any theory is whether it explains all the facts. So when doctrine develops, we should always look back at the Bible to check whether it is still in line with its foundations. And when Bible scholars discover new things through a better understanding of the languages, context, and meaning of the text, this should help theologians develop their theories. But too often, theology hardens into dogma, so that new facts are distrusted as a potential source of heresy.

My conviction is that knowing what the original readers were thinking helps us understand the issues the Bible's authors were addressing, which in turn helps us to formulate doctrine. My specialty is early Judaism in New Testament times, which I study in order to better understand the New Testament. Unfortunately, the early rabbis were not much interested in writing down their theology; they were more interested in how to keep God's law. Nevertheless, we can infer a great deal from their writings as well as from other ancient writings. We may not understand what the original authors were if we don't know which doctrines they were combating or what debates they were engaging with. For example, we will find that one reason Jesus spoke so often about the two paths to either heaven or hell was that Jews in his day believed there were three possible paths beyond death.

In this book, I'm asking how biblical studies can inform theology, because I believe we need to keep these two specialties talking to each other. Each of the following chapters deals with what we can learn about a particular doctrine if we try to get into the minds of the Bible's original readers. My choices of what to include reflect mainly what is being discussed in Christian communities at present. This usually means that they have traveled a long way from their origins in the Bible and may have changed significantly during the journey.

Because I concentrate on the foundations of doctrines, I admit that I can tend to neglect the centuries of valuable work done by theologians, most of whom are just as interested in the Bible as I am. However, while I may lack the nuance and knowledge of history that many theologians have, I still think biblical studies can make important contributions to doctrine. If we allowed our knowledge of the original context of Scripture to inform our doctrines—even established ones—what would we find?

I know that will sound unusual, if not dangerous, to someone who is well-versed in the development of doctrine. Perhaps I can blame my heritage as a Baptist. Since the Baptist church started as a back-to-the-Bible movement, we aren't generally keen on church tradition as a source of information. In spite of this, doctrines are a really valuable way to study the Bible. As you'll find, they can lead us to veins of unexplored Bible treasures that help us expand our knowledge and explore deeper into those doctrines, and into the mind and message of God.

Some doctrines are more important than others. We don't need to know lots of doctrines before God forgives our sins, but we do need to know something! In the last section I'll look at the doctrines that we should all agree on, but the other sections deal with those we can agree to disagree about. Many of them cause confusion and create debate, but unfortunately some result in unnecessary divisions. My hope for this book is that we will be able to understand other Christians better by understanding the biblical foundations for some of these doctrines that divide us.

1

▼

Finding Doctrine in the Bible Is Difficult

Doctrines summarize what the Bible says on different topics. But how do our conclusions today compare with those of the Bible's original readers? Understanding what they would have thought sometimes adds depth to our doctrine, but at other times it suggests there are things we have misunderstood.

Doctrines are the organized distillation of all the teaching of the Bible—in theory. In practice, as we'll discover, they don't always reflect the message of the Bible. Doctrines don't include history, geography, or other areas of knowledge that the Bible includes incidentally. They are only concerned with God and his interaction with humans and the rest of creation, because these are what the message of the Bible is about. However, doctrines now taught in our churches are often rather more complicated than what we find in the Bible.

For example, the traditional Christian doctrine of God—which includes attributes such as omnipotence, unchangeability, and timelessness—is based more on an ancient Greek model of absolutes than on the Bible. The Bible doesn't say much that defines the nature of God, and naturally we want to fill in these gaps. In many areas that theologians and ordinary believers long to know about, the Bible is virtually silent—such as the nature of heaven and hell, ways to predict the end of the world, how to obtain miracles of healing, or the spirit world of angels and demons.

In other matters, the Bible is by no means silent, though it can be confusing and apparently contradictory. These include topics such as human freedom and responsibility, how Jesus' crucifixion dealt with human sin, and precisely who goes to heaven.

The main reason for uncertainty in doctrines is that the Bible contains very little explicit theological teaching. It is mostly filled with things such as narrative, regulations for the nation of Israel, and poetry. We can learn a great deal about how God dealt with people in the past from these narratives, and the various regulations can (with care) tell us the moral directions in which God is nudging humanity. The Gospels' use of Jewish parables and enigmatic sayings makes them difficult to interpret. The poetry consists of prayers directed to God (mostly in the Psalms) and messages from God through prophets, which are largely warnings and pleas for repentance. Among these are many precious nuggets that tell us what God is like and how he runs the universe, but they aren't drawn together into coherent teaching. The New Testament letters are a more promising source of theology, though even these are mostly concerned with local matters in various churches.

If we regard the Bible as God's primary method of revealing himself to humanity, we have to conclude that he is not really interested in teaching us theology. This might seem flippant, but it is worth thinking about. We should at least acknowledge that doctrines don't communicate or engage nearly as effectively as a story, or poetry, or even a series of letters. We should also admit that most of the subjects we are interested in—the future, the spiritual world, and how God works in this world—aren't as important as what most of the Bible actually does address: our relationships with God and with each other.

We need to admit that creating Christian theology often fills in the gaps left in the Bible by extrapolating from what we know and trying to make sense of it. This involves imposing a coherent and logical system onto those hints found in the Bible. When we succeed in finding a pattern that fits, we should, like scientists, have the humility to call it a working theory. There may, of course, be more than one theory that incorporates all the facts in a coherent way. Throughout history, the church has tended to call rival theories "heresy" and excommunicate anyone who disagrees, which severely stifles dialogue!

The aim of this book is to demonstrate a method for exploring theology in the Bible. It is based on two main premises: (1) that there are a few core doctrines that we can be certain about (such as the Trinity, and salvation in the death and resurrection of Jesus) among many others that we can't; and (2) that the Bible is the one undisputed source of knowledge for theology. The main difference between this and other books on doctrine is the way in which the Bible is explored.

THE BIBLE THROUGH NEW EYES

Reading the Bible is very difficult for us, because we understand it through a lens that is colored by our church background and discussions of doctrines throughout history. For example, when we come across a description of God as sovereign, we immediately think about debates surrounding predestination or God's power and planning. However, when the original readers of the Bible text saw the word "sovereign," they thought of a sovereign—that is, a king—and they recognized that God was being compared to a human ruler. So instead of thinking of theological categories, they considered issues such as how far his rule extends, how glorious his throne room is, and how fair his laws are.

In this book I will attempt to look at doctrines through the lens of the original readers of the Bible. This is important because they are the people that the Bible was written for, and the human authors were attempting to communicate God's message to them—not to us. They wrote in ancient languages, using ancient metaphors and referring to ancient events as present-day occurrences, so we cannot expect to grasp the full meaning at first glance. Therefore, when biblical writers express an idea, we have to try to put ourselves in the place of the original readers in order to understand that idea.

WHAT WERE THEY TRYING TO SAY?

Theoretically, what we want to do can seem impossible. Many scholars of literature would say that it is actually impossible to know the "authorial intent"—that is, what the author was thinking about and intending to convey in their writing. This rather pessimistic conclusion is based on the fact that it is so easy to misunderstand an email from someone you meet every day, or even to misinterpret someone speaking to your face—even if you are married to them. You can mistake irony for plain speech, misunderstand who or what they are talking about, interpret advice as criticism, or even misunderstand the meaning of a word—for example, "that's incredible" ("amazing" or "unbelievable"?), "that's confusing" (a reference to what they describe, or the way they're describing it?), "*How* much?" ("too much" or "too little"?). Broken marriages and friendships testify to the difficulty of communicating. When you add the fact that an author is from a different family and area, possibly from a different culture, language, country, religion, and time period, there are so many possibilities for misunderstanding that some have concluded we can never be sure what the author meant.

The biggest barrier of all is that we can't look inside the mind of anyone—not even the person looking into our eyes. We cannot know what they are thinking (are they being pessimistic or optimistic about a situation?) or even be sure about how they are feeling (are they excited or anxious?). This is a much more serious problem when we can't see them, because there's only so much that an emoticon can communicate. So when we read something by someone we have never met, and we don't know what they were going through at the time they wrote it, it is impossible to interpret their words in the light of their feelings and current experiences. As a result, focusing on authorial intent leaves us with a host of problems.

HOW WAS IT UNDERSTOOD?

Fortunately there is a way forward: by looking at the *reception* of a message. If an author knows their readers, they should be able to write a message that will be received clearly—at least by those people they are writing for. So, in order to understand this message clearly, we have to find out as much as we can about the original readership and read the message through their eyes. This is difficult, and it won't be foolproof, but it isn't impossible.

When we try to understand doctrines, there is another barrier that doesn't often arise in other forms of communication. We have to understand the theology that those original readers already accepted. The person communicating will know what they already believed, so the message will spend more time on those aspects where they disagree and need to be persuaded, and skim over the aspects that they already understand well. That is why the Gospels rarely bother to affirm that there is only one God, whereas the Epistles, which are directed to those living in Gentile lands, include reminders that other so-called gods are nothing (1 Cor 8:4; Eph 4:6; 2 Thess 2:4; 1 Tim 2:5). This also explains why the Bible never bothers to tackle atheism—because that idea was unthinkable.

FIRMER FOUNDATIONS

This book aims to reinvigorate the doctrinal basis of our faith. It isn't a compendium of all doctrines, or even an in-depth investigation into a small number of doctrines. It is a series of pointers to places where, by attempting to discover how the Bible text might have been understood by its original recipients, we might rediscover the basis of what we believe or make new discoveries that illuminate problems.

Sometimes we'll find that the verses on which doctrines stand originally meant something slightly different, so perhaps our doctrines are tilting a little too far on their foundations. Other times we will find new insights that add breadth to what we understand, so that those doctrines gain a broader and firmer foundation. And sometimes we'll search for the Bible foundation of a doctrine and discover it is missing!—usually because we misunderstood a verse and then forgot we had based a doctrine on it.

You may disagree with some things while reading this book—and I'm hoping that you do. The purpose of the book is not to convey the conclusions but the method. You might disagree because you bring details to the table that I have neglected, or you may interpret the intent of a verse differently and come to a different solution. Or you may simply start with different assumptions. Most importantly, you may have a better insight into how the original readers would have interpreted the Bible text, and thereby have a different conclusion about what the author was conveying to them.

The aim is to review and revive church doctrine by looking at the Bible text, and that is something that anyone can do—but please do this with humility, alongside and listening to other believers. The Bible was written to the whole body of believers, not just to us as individuals, and doctrines should be the teaching of the whole church.

For me, the best result of this book would be for the church to gain new insight into those doctrines that cause massive divisions between believers, sometimes based on very shaky foundations. Undoing two thousand years of humanity's tendency to bicker and split into rival groups won't happen as a result of one small book, but it is worth aiming at! We are often tempted to look down on those who have got it all wrong. When that happens we should recall Jesus' words about specks of dust and planks of wood (Matt 7:3–5; Luke 6:41–42). So when you discover something exciting and new in the Bible, it is worth discussing with others before proclaiming it from pulpits or blogs. I would love these chapters to result in a deeper understanding and appreciation of the theology of others. I'd hate for them to inspire a new denomination!

Section 1

▼

Doctrines That Divide

2

▾

The Role of Tradition

All churches accumulate traditions—even those that claim to have done away with them! Can they help us to interpret the Bible, or should we challenge some of them like Jesus did?

I recently met some traditional Salafi Muslims at their bookstall in a shopping center. Keen to dissociate themselves from extremist offshoots such as ISIS, they are part of a back-to-Qur'an movement that pays little regard to later Islamic traditions that rule most Muslims. I realized with some surprise that they are the Islamic equivalent of Christians like me who regard the Bible alone as authoritative and give little weight to later church tradition.

Other branches of Islam can also be compared to similar Christian traditions. Shi'ite Muslims have a hierarchical system similar to Catholics and Orthodox churches, with an ayatollah ruling like a pope or patriarch. In contrast, Sunni Muslims are more like Protestants because every mosque can be independent, though most are banded together into groups like Christian denominations. Sufi Muslims are the charismatics of Islam, worshiping with lots of music and often enthusiastic dancing. The Ahmadiyya sect believe that the Islamic Messiah arrived in 1835, rather like Jehovah's Witnesses, who think the second coming started in 1914.

Muslims follow not only the Qur'an, but also the Hadith—the traditions of leaders after Muhammad that were written in various collections. A few early collections are accepted by most Muslims, but others are specific to Shi'ites, or the various branches of Sunni Muslims, who all follow their own different traditions. The Salafites don't accept these traditions as authoritative guidance and rely only on the Qur'an. They follow principles such as refusing to vote in elections, because there are no elections mentioned in the Qur'an. They are like Christian groups who use the Bible alone for theology, without the addition of historical church traditions. Such groups include the Brethren, Baptists, or those Church of Christ congregations that refuse to use musical instruments because the New Testament does not mention them being used by any church. However, the Salafites, like these Christian groups, have gradually accumulated their own traditions.

These parallels aren't merely coincidental, because we see a similar pattern in other religious traditions, and these groups certainly aren't trying to copy each other. Jews in Jesus' day illustrated the same patterns. Like Catholics, Orthodox, and Anglicans, Sadducees had a hierarchy topped by a high priest, while the Pharisees were like many Protestants in that they were independent while being grouped in denomination-type schools. The Pharisees originated because they rejected the historic Sadducean traditions, choosing to regard the Scriptures (the Old Testament) as their only authority. However, they soon started accumulating their own traditions, and when these were finally collected together as a written text (the Mishnah, at about AD 200) their traditions had already grown to about the size of the Bible. Subsequent generations treated the Mishnah as if it had almost scriptural authority and wrote commentaries on it called Talmuds. In reaction to this, the Dead Sea community (and later

Karaite Jews) started new back-to-the-Bible movements that rejected the Pharisees' traditions. However, these movements too started collecting their own traditions. Of course, another person who rejected the Pharisees' traditions was Jesus.

Christians in the New Testament era based all their teachings on the words of the Old Testament as interpreted by Jesus, but soon after New Testament times they too started accumulating their own traditions. When the church thought—and argued—about what was in the New Testament, they wrote up their decisions as creeds and summarized doctrine and Bible interpretation in other documents. Eventually, various churches produced complete legal systems of canon law and prayer books that determined what should be said in church services.

So we can see that all Christian groups accumulate traditions—even those that think they don't. All church movements soon find the need for creeds or statements of faith. Sermons and prayers soon settle into recognizable styles and phrases, so you can literally tell what kind of church you are in with your eyes shut. And every church starts amassing a body of traditions that can be encapsulated in the statement "We've always done it this way."

JESUS WAS ANGRY

Jesus appeared to be vehemently against human traditions that become more important than the Bible. One of his loudest condemnations of the Pharisees was "You nullify the word of God by your tradition that you have handed down" (Mark 7:13). On that occasion his disciples were eating without having washed their hands. The rabbis had added this rule because Old Testament priests had to wash before eating in the Temple, so it was clearly what God wanted. A nice interpretation, but it wasn't very practical when farm workers had a lunch break. Jesus pointed out that these human rules don't just make life difficult but can even undermine God's law. He gave the example of a *corban* oath (popular at the time) that was equivalent to "I'll be damned if you ever get a penny from me" (Mark 7:11). You might say this kind of thing when you are angry and then take it back. But the Pharisees said that you'd made an oath, so it was made before God and it must be carried out: they must never again get any financial support from you. And, once people knew that this was how it was interpreted, it would be an easy way to get out of a financial obligation: you would simply "accidentally" make a hasty vow like this, and then you couldn't reverse it, so you had no further obligation. Therefore, if someone spoke an oath like this to his parents, he legally couldn't give them any financial help again. The Pharisees taught that the law of oaths trumps the law of honoring parents (Num 30:2; Exod 20:12), so even elderly relatives could be left stranded as paupers by their family. Jesus rightly pointed out that this human tradition undermined Scripture—the commandment to honor your parents.

Although they got things so wrong, I'd like to put in a good word for the Pharisees because their hearts were often in the right place. The motivation behind all these rules and regulations was a desire to please God. If God gave a commandment, they reasoned that they should make sure they never got even close to breaking it. For example, God said they shouldn't work on a Sabbath by laboring to gather wood or getting a fire started, and they obeyed this.

They also protected this command with a "fence"—that is, they decided to put strict rules in place to make sure no one *accidentally* broke God's command. The fence in this case was an additional rule that on a Sabbath you shouldn't light any fires at all, however small—not even lighting a lamp from an existing fire. They wanted to remove all the questions about how *much* labor was involved—was this an easy fire to light, or was it moderately easy, or did it in fact involve "labor," which was forbidden? They reasoned that the way to make sure no one did any labor lighting a fire was to forbid them lighting *any* fire at all. This fence was a protection that kept people from walking too near the cliff edge of actually breaking God's law. As a result, some modern Jews won't even use a light switch on a Sabbath because this creates a tiny spark. So if a Jew returned from synagogue on Friday afternoon to find his wife had forgotten to light the lamps before sunset, they had to spend the whole evening in darkness—probably arguing about traditions!

ONLY HUMAN

Traditions are a part of being human. In every church community, worship follows an order (even if it is theoretically without any specific order), dress code is predictable, and many people probably look up doctrines in creeds or statements before turning to Scripture. Recently I was shocked to see a man wearing a flat cap while leading worship. Then I realized that in most churches today we don't make women wear hats, so we shouldn't demand that men be bareheaded, seeing as both customs are based on the same text (1 Cor 11:2-7). However, I was uneasy when I heard of an Australian church barbecue having communion with burgers and beer instead of bread and wine. I realize that Jesus used normal food for this meal, and normal food is now different, but it still seems wrong for one big reason: it isn't traditional!

Most traditions are useful, or at least convenient and comfortable, but they become toxic when they are used as barriers to necessary change. If we base our beliefs on traditions rather than Scripture, we won't realize when our interpretation of Scripture has been colored by an old culture. The ascetic movement of the early church was a reaction against the sexual and materialist corruption in the increasingly depraved and declining Roman Empire. But that tradition continued long after the original reason for it was gone, and we have only recently reversed it by allowing exuberant worship and relaxed clothing back into churches.

All of us will read Scripture through the lens of our traditions—we can't help it. But we should *be aware* that we are doing this. We must accept that Christians are influenced by tradition as much as Muslims, Jews, and people of other faiths. And, of course, tradition isn't all bad—being wary of change can save us from being swayed by every novel idea. But our tradition can also "nullify the word of God" when it blinds us to the true meaning of the Bible simply because it is different from what we've "always" done.

In the end, Scripture always has to trump tradition if we want to live our lives according to God's revelation rather than a human-made religion. And that means that sometimes we have to admit that we've been reading the Bible through lenses colored by our traditions. We need to reexamine the text through the lenses of the original readers. It might lead us to revise some of our traditions ... but I'm still not sure about communion with beer and burgers. I think I'll keep my tradition-colored shades on, for that situation at least.

3

▾

Baptism

Jews baptized themselves every day, so baptism wasn't something new for the early Christians. However, John changed the Jewish practice completely, and Jesus changed it into an initiation. Today different beliefs about baptism divide the modern church—but these are changing again.

Two clergymen were trying to pin down what the other believed about baptism: "What if the person is immersed up to his neck? Is that enough?" asked the Anglican.

"No," said the Baptist.

"What about up to his eyebrows then?"

"No," insisted the Baptist.

"Well, what if only a tiny bit of his forehead remains dry?"

"No, of course not!"

"Ah," said the Anglican triumphantly. "So what you are saying is that the most important thing is to wet the forehead."

Despite all the bad jokes on the subject, there are no serious divisions in the church about the *method* of baptism. Those who use a few drops of water (like Anglicans and Catholics) don't have problems with immersion—they just don't think it is necessary. And those who do practice immersion will usually allow exceptions on grounds of health, which implies that they do not believe that full immersion is functionally necessary.

But what about the issue of *when* to baptize? Isn't that a huge bone of contention? Well, no; the church isn't really divided by this either. Those who baptize babies also baptize adults, and those who only baptize "believers" are often willing to baptize children who are so young that it is questionable whether they have truly decided for themselves.

What really divides the church is belief about what baptism *does*. Does it save individuals by admitting them into membership of the universal church, or does it proclaim their Christian commitment (which they have already made) in public?

Jews in Jesus' day understood and practiced baptism very differently. They baptized themselves most days. Houses excavated from that time usually have a baptism tank (called a *mikveh*) carved into the floor of the basement. This was a hole about the size of an upright coffin with steps into it. It wouldn't have been particularly clean; fresh water flowed into the top of it and overflowed into a drain, but this only really freshened the surface. Its purpose was to cleanse you from ceremonial impurities, rather than to wash off the dirt.

Impurity in Moses' law came from sexual activity, menstruation, and being under the same roof as a corpse (Lev 15; Num 19). You could also become impure by touching an impure person or by using something they had used—a chair or cup, for example—so it was almost impossible to avoid. According to the law, cleansing wasn't really necessary until you wanted to do something sacred such as eating a Passover meal or visiting the Temple. However, Jews in Jesus' day wanted to be holy at all times, so every day they stripped naked and immersed themselves in the *mikveh*.

I almost fell into one of these excavated holes. One rainy afternoon in Jerusalem several years ago, I went to look at the newly uncovered Temple steps. No one was around, and I am sorry to admit that I stepped over the rope—I just couldn't resist treading on the steps that Jesus had actually walked on. There were also new excavations of the foundations of various ancient buildings close by. I was just about to walk through a large puddle when I recognized its rectangular edges. I immediately pulled back, with my heart beating and visions of newspaper headlines saying "British Academic Hits Head and Drowns in First-Century *Mikveh*"!

JOHN THE REVOLUTIONARY BAPTIST

The way that John (the Baptist) baptized was revolutionary: it was done in public (so presumably the person wasn't naked); it was performed *by* someone (John); and it was for cleansing of sin—not for impurity. This was the first time someone had offered Jews a ceremony for marking repentance of moral sins, and it became immensely popular. The Temple sin offerings were for breaking specific laws, such as the Sabbath regulations; they didn't cover moral sins such as losing your temper with a colleague, or telling lies about him, or hitting him. These types of sin were dealt with by repentance, which later became effective on the Day of Atonement; but John's baptism gave Jews a way to mark that repentance immediately and very graphically.

Christians adopted John's baptism, but they also changed it. It was no longer important who performed the baptism (John 4:2), and it became a one-time initiation, rather than a regular cleansing from sins (Matt 28:19). This reinforced the distinction between Judaism and Christianity: the constantly repeated Temple sacrifices were replaced by the single sacrificial act of Jesus, and similarly the washing away of sin at baptism happened only once.

These changes introduced two problems: What if you sin after baptism? And are you saved if you die before baptism? The first was a big difficulty in the early church, because there was a widespread belief that any sins after baptism were unforgivable. For this reason many believers, such as Constantine, put off baptism till their deathbed, just in case. This is not a problem today, because forgiveness is no longer tied to the act of baptism, like it was when the ministry of John the Baptist was still a vivid memory. For us, it is obvious that further repentance can occur at any time and doesn't require the rite of baptism to accompany it. However, the second question has gained a huge importance because it divides the church: Do we need baptism for salvation?

Some churches believe that baptism enacts admission into the protection of the church, so it is important to baptize people as soon as possible and also baptize babies. Others understand it as a public proclamation of an individual's repentance, which means it should be delayed until that repentance has actually occurred.

Paul's view was this: "Don't you know that all of us who were baptized into Christ Jesus were baptized into his death? We were therefore buried with him through baptism into death in order that, just as Christ was raised from the dead ..." (Rom 6:3–4). This text is important to both sides—it can be used to affirm that the act of baptism confers new life, or it can affirm that baptism is the immersion of adults. However, its message to the original readers was something different, because they faced a different issue that is now ancient history.

FROM DEATH TO LIFE

When Gentiles became Jews, they were immersed in order to "separate [them] from the grave."[1] This phrase was used by Jews

---

1. Mishnah *Pesachim* 8:8 (TinyURL.com/Pesachim8-8). Note that this book shortens internet links using TinyURL.com to make them easier to type into the address bar of your browser.

to indicate that the person being baptized, like all Gentiles, suffered from death impurity. You could contract death impurity by entering any building where someone had died—which happened at some time or other in every public and private building. Jewish houses and buildings were cleansed after someone had died in them, but Gentile buildings weren't. This means that almost all Gentile buildings had permanent death impurity. If Jews had to go inside one, they carried out a simple purification ceremony, and after a week they were clean again (Num 19:11–12). But Gentiles didn't purify themselves, so every Gentile had picked up death impurity at some point. Converts therefore had to be cleansed from death impurity by immersion; otherwise they would bring this contamination into the Jewish community.

When Christians adopted baptism as their rite of admission, we can imagine that Jews taunted them about using a "baptism for death impurity," just as they taunted them about God's curse on any corpse that is hung from a tree (Deut 21:23). Paul answered the taunts about this curse by turning it into something positive: Yes, Jesus took "God's curse" for us (Deut 21:23; Gal 3:13). He did the same thing with the taunt about baptism and death impurity, saying: Yes, baptism *is* about death—we share the death *and resurrection* of Jesus (Rom 6:3–4).

The church later picked up this reference to resurrection and started teaching that new life starts at baptism. In the sixteenth century, Reformation theologians reasserted that salvation depended only on faith leading to repentance and not on baptism or other ceremonies. This created a permanent split in the church.

A few years ago, the Catholic Church revised its view significantly. In 2006 Pope Benedict XVI decreed that unbaptized babies do go to heaven and not to limbo. This reversed the belief affirmed as recently as 1905 by Pope Pius X that "children who die without baptism ... do not deserve paradise." Of course, this papal pronouncement hasn't completely undone the deep-seated division that is based on the belief that baptism is necessary for salvation. Catholic and Orthodox churches continue to baptize babies in the hope that they will confirm their repentance at a later date, while Nonconformist churches withhold baptism until that repentance occurs. Anglicans, in their special way, stand in the middle and do both.

But there is another remarkable ray of hope: most churches now recognize each other's baptisms. Some might say that aspects of a baptism carried out in a different church were "wrong," but more and more accept that a person is baptized in the eyes of God, even if the process was not the same in all the particulars. I think this represents a game-changing viewpoint, and we may find in heaven that many doctrinal differences such as this are merely human squabbles. That's how most non-Christians regard them, and perhaps they are right.

4

▼

Church Governance

Denominations use different systems of leadership, from powerful hierarchies to self-ruling congregations. The Bible isn't clear about leadership structures in the first churches, but there are some clues.

During the same week in November 2012, Americans voted for their president, the Chinese were informed about their new Politburo leaders, and Coptic Orthodox believers had the identity of their new pope revealed to them by a blindfolded boy who picked his name from the three laid on an altar. It was a rather nice quirk of timing that highlights the different ways in which nations and churches are governed.

Leadership styles divide the church now more than ever. The quaint method used by the Coptic church is actually the most Bible based, because this is roughly how the twelfth apostle was picked after Judas' death (Acts 1:23–26). Other churches rely either on voting by members (to varying degrees) or on the decision of existing leaders. This difference creates a dividing line that cuts deeper than theology, because of what it says about the value of individual members. It also creates a division between denominations that is difficult to bridge.

The Catholic and Orthodox churches are at one end of the spectrum, having strict hierarchies and a top-down chain of command. At the bottom-up end are churches such as the

Mennonites, who prefer to keep discussing until a unanimous consensus is possible. Between these extremes is a huge variety of leadership structures.

The church occasionally attempts to overcome such divisions. In 1972 the Congregational and Presbyterian churches of the UK decided to unite because they were theologically identical in almost all respects except church government: Congregationalist members voted on all big decisions, while decisions were made by the presbytery (regional elected elders) on the Presbyterian members' behalf. The two denominations merged to become the United Reformed Church, with the agreement that congregations would vote on local matters, while the elders would vote on regional and national issues. This was hailed as a significant reversal in the Protestant tendency toward divisions and subdivisions. Unfortunately, several congregations from both sides disagreed with the compromise and refused to be a part of the United Reformed Church, so the two denominations merged and became three!

WHAT'S IN A NAME?

As with most church divisions, disagreement about church leadership largely occurs because of Scripture's lack of clarity on the subject. The New Testament names several titles, many of which we still use, and their Greek and Latin forms are also used in church terminology: deacon (Greek *diakonos*; Latin *minister*), elder (Greek *presbyteros*), bishop (Greek *episkopos*), shepherd (Latin *pastor*), and father (Greek and Latin *pater*, or intimately *papa*). The term "apostle" is only used in a few churches because it referred to the church's founders and occasionally to actual "messengers" (Phil 2:25; 2 Cor 8:23). "Shepherd" is used only once for people other than Jesus and appears to be a role rather than a title (Eph 4:11). And according to Acts, "elders" are the same as "bishops" (Acts 20:17, 28).

This leaves two main categories of early church leaders: deacons and elders/bishops. We might want to conclude that this demonstrates clearly that the standard leadership structure of the early church was based on these two types of leaders. But if this was the case, we would expect the two types to occur regularly together, whereas, in fact, deacons (often translated "servants") are mentioned just once with elders and once with bishops (often translated "overseers")—in 1 Timothy 3 and Philippians 1:1. Unfortunately, the only clear pattern in the Bible is that deacons occur mostly in Paul's writings and elders occur mostly elsewhere.

The likely explanation for this confusion is that church governance was still evolving in New Testament times, so different terms and structures were used in different times and places. By the end of the first century, however, writings such as Didache and First Clement clearly reflect a dual structure of deacons and elders, and, a little later, Ignatius assumes that several elders submit to a single bishop. As time went on, in the Latin church, the Greek word for elder was replaced by the Latin word for priest (*sacerdos*), and the Greek word for bishop was replaced with the Latin *popa*. Finally the *popa* of Rome became the Catholic pope, while others became patriarchs of various Orthodox churches.

A DISAPPEARING WATCH

Which system works best? Both appointments from the top and voting by church members can produce heroic and also disastrous leaders. When the elderly John XXIII was appointed as a caretaker pope in 1958, no one predicted that he would put in motion the most important modernization of the Catholic

Church. The Second Vatican Council encouraged lay involvement in worship and Bible studies, the use of modern languages
in the Mass instead of Latin, and replacing private confessionals
with collective prayers.

The head of the Russian Orthodox Church since 2009, Patriarch Kirill I, has a rather different track record. When he was
seen wearing a $30,000 watch in a website photograph, he
denied it was true, and certainly the watch was no longer visible when people rechecked the site. However, the highly reflec-
tive table at which he was sitting in the photo retained a clear
image of the now-missing watch![1] And, in support of Russian
President Vladimir Putin, he pulled the whole Russian church
out of the Ecumenical Patriarchate when it recognized the inde-
pendence of Ukraine.

Democratic church governance can go just as badly wrong
when church members expect their leaders to cater to their
desires. For example, just before the calendars ticked over from
1999 to 2000, one pastor was voted out of his job by church members who complained that he refused to preach warnings about
the coming world disaster called the Millennium Bug (remember that nonevent?).

My own selection for the ministry was not, I hope, typical.
When I applied to a Baptist college, the administration asked
my church and minister whether they recommended me for
the ministry. The question was brought to the church meeting
to be voted on. As I was relatively new in the area, not many
church members knew who I was. However, at a recent church
party I had organized a game where the winner was the person
able to pronounce the words "chubby bunnies" with the most

---

1. Michael Schwirtz, "$30,000 Watch Vanishes Up Church Leader's Sleeve"
(TinyURL.com/Kirill-watch).

marshmallows stuffed into their mouth. So the church meeting was asked: "Do you recommend David for the ministry? You know—the one who entertained us with chubby bunnies!" All their hands went up. Hmmm ...

Nevertheless, ballots are a good way to help the silent majority have their say and hopefully to let common sense outweigh either improper influence or extremism. The Bible doesn't tell us which system of church governance is best, but it does affirm the concerted opinion of the body of believers. According to Jesus, the whole congregation should be the final arbiter in matters of church discipline (Matt 18:17). The first deacons were chosen by the body of believers before being "appointed" by the apostles (Acts 6:1–6). There is even a hint in Acts 14:23 that elders were elected by the congregation, because the word most Bibles translate as "appoint" is actually the normal Greek word for "to vote."

Personally, I think it is wise to use some system of voting by the congregation to establish leaders. I especially like the double-vote system when choosing a minister, as it encourages unity. In the first vote, everyone supports whomever they prefer best. In the second vote, everyone considers whether God was speaking through the majority and whether they could affirm that choice. This often results in a unanimous vote—which is a wonderful way to start a ministry!

5

▼

The Rapture

Belief in the rapture arose from a couple of ambiguous prophecies to become a necessary article of faith for many. Perhaps we can't work out what prophecy means in advance, but then, what is its purpose?

I t was the 1960s—and many Christians felt that the world was spiraling out of control. The sexual revolution and an imminent war of mutual assured destruction made it feel like the end was coming soon. Eschatology—the study of the second coming and the end times—became a hot Christian topic.

As a teenager during that time, I loved the detailed charts of end-time chronology, with their clear predictions about military deployments and political allegiances. I had a problem with Jesus' saying that we can't know the day or the hour of his coming (Matt 24:36), but a Bible teacher assured me that Jesus didn't say we couldn't know the year! Every now and then over the years a specific prophecy seemed to have been fulfilled—only to falter subsequently. In 1981, for example, the tenth nation joined the European Union—a thrilling match to the number of horns on Revelation's beast (Rev 17:12). Now, however, there are many more member nations (but perhaps the UK has started a countdown back to ten!). Likewise, in 1986 the disaster at Chernobyl (which means "wormwood" in Ukrainian) contaminated rainfall all over Europe (see Rev 8:11); however, this didn't result in multitudes dying.

In that time of uncertainty, many preachers consulted the works of teachers such as J. N. Darby, C. I. Scofield, and Charles Ryrie and discovered something wonderful: the church would be "raptured"—taken off the planet—seven years before the second coming. This doctrine taught that although things would get increasingly bad, Christians wouldn't have to endure the worst times at the end. It was a powerful evangelistic message that galvanized multitudes into making a decision for Christ in case they missed the lift. The popularity of the book series *Left Behind*—later made into a TV series and a movie—shows that it is still a powerful message.

But beliefs about the timing of the rapture created new divisions in the church. Doctrinal statements started to include "pretribulation rapture" among the foundational beliefs of many churches and colleges, especially in the US. This caused other institutions to add opposing positions to their statements. Often staff and students had to sign their agreement to a particular stance—and many still do—as if belief about the rapture is as important as belief in the resurrection. Perhaps it became foundational because many supporters came to Christ as a result of preaching on this topic. But should we insist that everyone believe the same on this point? In the UK we now avoid this division in a very British way—by not talking about it.

So will Christians have to suffer the terrible times that precede Christ's second coming, or will they be raptured?

SIGNS OF THE END

If you are looking for signs of the end, you will find that virtually every news bulletin seems to include at least one war, famine, or earthquake. Jesus listed these three signs in his answer to the question "What will be the sign of your coming and of the end of the age?" (Matt 24:3). However, when you read the text, you find that these signs are merely "the beginning of birth pains," so Jesus added, "see to it that you are not alarmed." Instead of getting ready for an imminent end when these signs appear, Jesus told his disciples that "such things must happen, but the end is still to come" (24:6).

Much of what Jesus said in these prophecies was in answer to the other question that the disciples asked at the same time. Jesus had just told them about the destruction of the Jerusalem Temple, so they asked him two questions, "When will this happen?" and "What signs will there be?" That is, they asked him about two completely separate sets of events, which they understandably thought were the same: the destruction of the Temple and the "end," when Jesus will return. So part of Jesus' answer relates to the destruction of Jerusalem and its Temple in AD 70, and part to his return in the future, and it can be tricky deciding which is which.

There is only one sign in Matthew 24 that is unquestionably a sign of the end, because it is immediately followed by the words "and then the end will come." It is "this gospel of the kingdom will be preached in the whole world as a testimony to all nations" (Matt 24:14). That's a news headline we haven't seen yet, but many people are working toward that aim. This helps to explain why Christians are left on the earth after they are saved: they are supposed to share their discovery with others.

LEFT BEHIND?

This realization about Jesus' teaching makes me very uneasy about the pretribulation rapture, because it leaves the earth without any Christian witness. In the *Left Behind* series, many do recognize God's action behind the disappearance of so many people and turn to him as a result, but that's just a nice story. I am also uneasy about the rapture because it gives Christians a "get-out-of-suffering-free" card. By contrast, Jesus said that his disciples must "take up their cross" (Matt 10:38 = Luke 9:23) and that "the one who stands firm to the end will be saved" (Matt 24:13), which suggests that the faithful will not be rescued before the end.

The text that encapsulated the rapture for me and many others was the repeated phrase "one will be taken and the other left" in Luke 17:34–35. Perhaps it was so memorable because the accompanying words of the King James Version inevitably provoked a snigger from the youth group: "There shall be two men in one bed ... two women shall be grinding together." At that time I didn't realize that in Greek literature the passive verb "taken" can mean "captured,"[2] which makes a lot of sense in the context. Jesus urged Judean believers to flee to the hills (vv. 31–33); otherwise they would be "taken" by the soldiers (Luke 21:20–21).

In Revelation, heaven is certainly full of people who have come out of the tribulation, but they have done so by being killed (Rev 6:11; 7:14; 13:15; 14:13). John doesn't mention anyone who was rescued from harm. And when Paul says that believers will "meet the Lord in the air," they are those "who are left until the coming of the Lord"—so they aren't saved from suffering before his coming (1 Thess 4:15–17).

THE MEANING OF PROPHECY

I finally realized that I'd stopped believing in a pretribulation rapture when I came across AfterTheRapturePetCare.com[3] and

---

2. E.g., those "taken" by Hannibal in Polybius's *Histories* 3.69.2 (TinyURL. com/Polybius-3-69).

3. TinyURL.com/Petcare-Rapture.

I was able to laugh about it. This service is provided by kindly non-Christians who offer to collect your pets and care for them after you have disappeared—for a small up-front fee.

I've also now given up trying to predict the future from Scripture. No one can fathom the meaning of prophecy before it happens. Think of the Old Testament prophecies about Jesus: they are easy to recognize in retrospect, but it was almost impossible before Jesus came. For example, Psalm 22 doesn't say that it is describing the death of the Messiah, but with hindsight we can see amazing predictions about Jesus' crucifixion: "They pierce my hands and my feet. ... They ... cast lots for my garment" (vv. 16, 18). However, it also contains details such as: "Many bulls surround me. ... Lions ... open their mouths at me" (vv. 12–13)—which make it sound as if Jesus was killed in an arena by wild animals! We can now recognize these details as metaphorical, but in advance it wasn't possible to see which details were literal and which were symbolic. In the same way, we can't know in advance which aspects of prophecies about the end will turn out to be literal or symbolic. Will Jerusalem be surrounded by literal armies or metaphorical ones? Will Jesus arrive on a literal horse? We can make guesses about things like this, but should recognize that we are likely to get things wrong.

So what's the purpose of prophecy? Jesus told his disciples just before his death: "I have told you now before it happens, so that when it does happen you will believe" (John 14:29). Predictions in prophecy are mainly for those who will experience the predicted events. If we are still alive when the end times come, we may even find that *every* interpretive guess about these prophecies was wrong! All the pieces will fall into place, and the meaning will become obvious, but it won't be what we thought. Even though the world will be falling apart around us, we will recognize that the details were already in God's word.

And, because of those prophecies, we'll be strengthened for the coming trouble, knowing that the end is ultimately in God's hands.

6

▾

Free Will

Do we choose God or does he choose us? We can reason either way from the Bible depending on how we understand certain words. What we believe about free will shapes the way we describe what God is like.

A few days before Barack Obama's reelection as US president, new statistics showed a rise in the number of jobs, though simultaneously the number registered as unemployed also rose because more people had signed on to seek work. Obama greeted this as a sign that the economy was recovering, while his rivals took it as proof that the economy was stagnant. But while we expect politicians to put their spin on facts, are we guilty of doing the same when it comes to interpreting the Bible?

The issue of predestination is a case in point. Some Christians believe that God decides who will be saved, while others believe that we can freely choose to follow or reject God. Both stances can be validated in Scripture. The first group (Calvinists) emphasize Bible words such as "predestined," "chosen," and "elect" to support their view; those with the opposing view emphasize "repent," "follow," and "believe." These two competing systems of theology now divide the church.

John Calvin, an influential French theologian in the sixteenth century, developed a self-consistent Bible-based theology based on the assumption that God is totally in charge. This means that when someone chooses to follow God, they are in fact doing what God had already planned for them. Later, a Dutch theologian, Jacobus Arminius, responded with an equally self-consistent and Bible-based theology based on the assumption that God allows people to have real freedom of choice. Today this theology is often called "Wesleyan" after John Wesley, who refined it in the eighteenth century.

RIVAL THEORIES

Although these two systems contradict each other, both are Bible-based—they both take the Bible seriously, but they understand some Bible words differently. Take, for example, the New Testament word that we translate as "predestination" (Greek *proorizō*—i.e., "prior-plan"). Calvinists regard this as God's inescapable prior planning to provide salvation for some and condemnation for others, while Wesleyans regard it as God's prior planning to provide salvation for everyone, which they have to accept or reject. Similarly, "election" and "calling" are understood differently in each system. Calvinists apply them to selected individuals whom God has invited, while Wesleyans apply them to everyone because they say that God has saved and invited everyone, though only some accept.

When the word "sovereignty" is used—that is, God's kingly ability to do whatever he wishes—there is a very subtle distinction. Wesleyans say that whatever God wants to happen will happen, whereas Calvinists say that whatever happens is what God wants to happen. The distinction lies in the way that human choice is carried out. Wesleyans think that God wants humans to freely choose him, but Calvinists think this free choice must be directed by God, because otherwise it could override God's will.

Key Bible verses are understood differently by both systems. Wesleyans quote proof verses such as "God our Savior, who wants all people to be saved and ... Christ Jesus, who gave himself as a ransom for all people" (1 Tim 2:3-6). Calvinists say that this can't actually mean "all people" because in that case God's will has been be thwarted when some people rejected him. Therefore, for Calvinists, the phrase "all people" must mean "all [kinds of] people."

Calvinists quote verses such as "those God foreknew he also predestined" (Rom 8:29) and "he predestined us for adoption ... in accordance with his purpose and will" (Eph 1:5). In reply, Wesleyans point out that "foreknow" implies that God *knows* beforehand, rather than *decides* beforehand. They also say that since Roman adoption normally involved a young adult who had to agree to be adopted, Paul's picture implies human choice— that is, God wants to adopt everyone, but only some respond and agree to become his children.

In the Gospels, Jesus' words appear to support both sides. He says that "many are invited, but few are chosen" (Matt 22:14), which seems to imply that only the chosen few will be saved. However, he accompanied this with a parable that turned the saying on its head. In the parable of the banquet, a king invited chosen guests to his banquet, but they declined, so he called for everyone else to come. We get a similarly double-sided message in the parables of the lost in Luke 15: the prodigal decided by himself to return, but the stray sheep was sought and carried back. Jesus' teaching is clearly neither Calvinist nor Wesleyan— he portrays the truths of both understandings: God seeks and brings us back, and also we decide to return.

"WHOEVER COMES TO ME"

This balance is displayed especially in John 6:37, where it appears that the first clause supports Calvinism and the second clause supports Wesleyanism: "All those the Father gives me will come to me; and whoever comes to me I will never drive away." However, as with other such verses, both sides have a reasonable explanation to affirm their own view. Some Calvinists say the first clause is God's viewpoint and the second is a human viewpoint. Other Calvinists say that the order is important: first God chooses who will come to Jesus, and then Jesus accepts those who come. Wesleyans counter that if the order is important, the process must start with human choice because Jesus began this section in verse 35, saying "Whoever comes to me ..."

Does the church really need to be divided by these opposing interpretations? Perhaps we can cut through the arguments by applying common sense. Do we feel free or do we feel controlled? Even this question doesn't have a clear-cut solution. Sometimes we feel like a puppet manipulated by circumstances, as if God and the universe are pushing us around. At other times we feel as if we have at least some freedom—like any toddler who refuses to eat their vegetables or share a toy, we can choose to do or not do things. Wesleyans may feel that this bolsters their position, but again, this isn't decisive because extreme Calvinists say that God makes us *feel* free, and moderate Calvinists say that we use real freedom to choose what God planned.

Having read this, you may be concluding that New Testament authors didn't want to express certainty on this point, because they appear to be totally equivocal. It is difficult to be sure, but this is probably close to the truth, because it seems that Jews at the time were similarly divided and uncertain. Rabbi Akiva put it most succinctly at the end of the first century, saying: "Everything is foreseen; yet free will is given."[1] This viewpoint from two angles is as close as early Christians could get to understanding

---

1. Pirkei Avot 3.15 (TinyURL.com/P-Avot-3).

how God worked, and it appears that they were satisfied with that position.

Personally I lean toward the Wesleyan point of view because this describes God as I know him: his fundamental characteristic is love—so, he enacts his love to everyone by saving and inviting us all. Calvinists regard God's fundamental characteristic as justice, so he shows grace towards only the few whom he has decided to save. However, if God's overarching characteristic were justice rather than love, I would expect him to punish us all or have grace toward us all. I have difficulty with the Calvinist view that a righteous God decides to punish some individuals for their sins and decides to save others (by causing them to repent) even though they were equally sinful. I can see that you could call this gracious (because there is no need for God to save anyone), but you could also call it unfair.

You might well quote Paul's words to me: "But who are you ... to talk back to God? 'Shall what is formed say to the one who formed it, "Why did you make me like this?"'" (Rom 9:20). However, although God hardened Pharaoh's heart (vv. 17-18), Pharaoh also hardened it himself (see Exod 9:34-35). That is, Pharaoh decided to be obstructive, and God helped him stick to that decision because it worked well for God's plan for the nations.

In the end, I respect both systems of theology, except for the extremes. Extreme Calvinists may not bother to communicate the gospel because they believe that those whom God has chosen will come to him, whatever we do. Extreme Wesleyans may also neglect spreading the gospel because they think that neither sin nor the devil can interfere with human freedom to believe in God. When any theology discourages us from sharing God's love with others, we know it has gone wrong.

Political parties flounder when they have divisions, and the gospel can be similarly damaged by theological divisions. Wesley had an acrimonious and public dispute with fellow evangelist George Whitefield, who championed a Calvinist interpretation. However, Wesley's funeral oration for Whitefield contains the first recorded use of what is now a commonplace phrase that I'd love to hear Christians say to each other more often: "We may agree to disagree."

7

▾

Inerrancy

Does the Bible contain contradictions, inexact measures, and perhaps actual errors? And, if so, does this mean that the Bible isn't real history?

There's something about coming to the end of a film or book and finally understanding the baffling details that have previously made no sense. Different incidents are explained, problems are ironed out, and everything comes to a satisfactory ending. But viewers or readers hate stories that conclude with unanswered questions and inconsistencies, so editors try to eradicate any such untidiness. So well-edited books leave no loose ends and contain no contradictions.

Critics of the Bible sometimes mistake it for this kind of literature. They know the claim that the Bible is inspired by God (2 Tim 3:16), so they think that its narrative should be tidy, self-explanatory, and self-consistent. However, ancient historians know that potential contradictions and apparent mistakes are normal in true historical documents, so they aren't surprised to find them in the Bible. In fact, if there weren't any inconsistencies or problems, historians would conclude that it was either made up or overedited in order to "correct" it. Anyway, historians *love* problems and difficult details, because these can often lead to the discovery of hidden events and new historical facts.

This doesn't mean that Bible scholars are not interested in getting to the bottom of difficulties in the text. They investigate them keenly, and every now and then a mystery is solved by new information. For instance, Genesis 2:14 locates Eden in eastern Turkey, at the heads of the Euphrates and Tigris rivers. That was a problem because both ancient and modern thought placed the origin of humanity elsewhere. We expected Eden to be in Africa or perhaps in ancient Mesopotamia, where human culture first produced towns and agriculture. However, recent excavations at Göbekli Tepe in eastern Turkey reveal a sophisticated worship center two thousand years older than the Mesopotamian civilization. And on nearby hills, geneticists have pinpointed the origin of the grass from which all varieties of cultivated wheat have descended.[1] In other words, the earliest evidence of human worship and farming is in the area of the biblical Eden. This doesn't mean that we have found the identity of Eden, but the geographic clues in the Bible now agree with clues from other disciplines.

PROBLEMS SOLVED

Sometimes new discoveries create problems before they solve them. There was no archaeological evidence for the name "Nazareth" until it was found in 1960 on an inscription. But, surprisingly, the name was spelled *Natsereth*, with the Hebrew letter *tsade* instead of the letter *za'in* as implied by the Greek Gospels. However, these two letters are very similar—they are both versions of "z." The difference in pronunciation is similar to the difference between the tower of "Pisa" and the food "pizza,"

---

1. See Asle Rønning, "On the Track of the World's First Farmer" (TinyURL. com/FirstFarmer).

though of course we aren't sure how they were pronounced in first-century Palestine.

Now that we know "Nazareth" was spelled with a *tsade* instead of *zayin*, this actually solves the problem of the quote "He shall be called a Nazarene" (Matt 2:23). There is no prophecy in the Old Testament about the Messiah being a Nazer (i.e., someone who takes a Nazirite vow), but there *are* prophecies about him being a Natser (i.e., a "Branch," as in Isa 11:1). So this solution, which had been guessed by many commentators, is now confirmed by archaeology.

Although factual problems are sometimes resolved by new discoveries, the Bible still contains many issues for biblical scholars to puzzle over. For example, Mark 2:26 says David ate the holy bread reserved for priests "in the days of Abiathar the high priest." But 1 Samuel 21:1-4 says it was the priest Ahimelek who gave David this bread. Commentators have come up with some ingenious solutions. Perhaps Abiathar was the high priest at the time that Ahimelek handed over this bread—because in this passage Ahimelek was merely called a "priest." This would be credible if the high priest Abiathar had been the father of Ahimelek, but actually it was the other way around—Abiathar was the son of Ahimelek (1 Sam 22:20). Or perhaps "in the days of" simply means "in the days of his lifetime," indicating that Abiathar was already born. This solution works fine in English, but the words "days of" don't actually occur in the Greek, which simply has *epi*. In this kind of context, *epi* is the normal way to express "during the tenure/reign of," as in "during the high-priesthood of Annas" (Luke 3:2).

The real answer is probably that Abiathar was well known and Ahimelek wasn't. Abiathar figures a great deal in the story of David—in fourteen separate chapters—whereas only this one event is recorded for the whole life of Ahimelek, so Abiathar was named, even though this wasn't exactly correct. This wasn't intended to fool anyone, but it was intended to be helpful.

We often do the same kind of thing. For example, we might say, "In the days of President Kennedy the Russians started the space race, but the Americans eventually won it." Strictly speaking this is wrong, because the Russians launched Sputnik in 1957 and Kennedy's presidency started in 1961, but that doesn't really make the statement false—it is merely wrong in a small detail. In the same way, Mark says that David ate the priests' bread back in the day of that famous high priest Abiathar, though Abiathar didn't actually become high priest till his father was killed a few months later.

APPROXIMATE MEASURES

The Bible approximates in other ways. For example, 1 Kings 7:23 says the round temple basins were ten cubits across and thirty cubits around. However, pi is 3.14, so if the diameter was ten cubits, the circumference must have been 31.4 cubits. Some interpreters suggest that diameter was measured below the rim, where it was narrower, which could be the solution. But it seems more likely that the author didn't intend to make exact measurements. There are more than two hundred occasions where things are measured in "cubits" (i.e., the length from the hand to the elbow), but a fraction of a cubit occurs only for the frame, table, and ark of the covenant in the Tabernacle, and the height of Goliath is "six cubits and a span" (Exod 25:10, 17, 23; 26:16; 1 Sam 17:4). Perhaps all the other lengths were really exact multiples of a cubit, but it seems more likely that the Bible is recording sensible approximations.

But if the authors of Bible books approximate sometimes, how can we know when they are being accurate? Can we rely on every detail in the Bible? The most authoritative Protestant answer to this question is the Chicago Statement on Biblical Inerrancy (1978), which says: "Scripture, having been given by divine inspiration, is infallible, so that ... it is true and reliable in all the matters it addresses" (article XI). The Chicago Statement does allow for the possibility that scribes might occasionally have made a copying error (article X), and it says that we should not judge Scripture by "standards of truth and error that are alien to its usage and purpose ... lack of modern technical precision ... use of hyperbole" (see article XIII). Nevertheless, "inspiration, though not conferring omniscience, guaranteed true and trustworthy utterance on all matters" (article IX).[2] This statement is not a simplistic conclusion that everything in the Bible is true as stated because it takes into account that the Bible is not a technical manual with exact measurements and that it often uses poetic exaggeration or metaphor.

In practice, many Protestants follow the principle that the Bible is accurate concerning its main message (i.e., God's relationship with humanity and our salvation) and not necessarily accurate with regard to incidental details that occur. Roughly the same conclusion was reached by the Second Vatican Council in 1964 on the inerrancy of Scripture. Catholic statements used to be very similar to the Chicago Statement. For example, Pope Leo XIII said in 1893, "It is absolutely wrong and forbidden ... to admit that the sacred writer has erred," and he criticized those who limited divine inspiration to "the things of faith and morals, and nothing beyond." But the Second Vatican Council came to a different conclusion because it considered problems such as Abiathar and Ahimelek (discussed above) and Matthew 27:9, which quotes words from "Jeremiah" that actually occur in Zechariah 11:12–13. It concluded that inerrancy was indeed limited to

2. TinyURL.com/ChicagoBelief.

matters of faith and morals—the intrinsic message of God. In order to not contradict Leo XIII, the final statements emphasized the subtle difference between inspiration (i.e., originating from God) and inerrancy (i.e., containing no errors), though I'm not sure Leo XIII would have agreed with this distinction.[3]

WHAT TO DO WITH APPARENT CONTRADICTIONS

God has chosen to communicate his word through fallible humans, and everyone agrees that these human authors are reflected in their various writing styles. Most would also accept that these authors could make errors in grammar without affecting the truth of the message. So, why shouldn't the same apply to occasional errors in fact? So long as the message is still clear, why would God allow one type of insignificant error and not another?

Since God inspired humans to write in their own style instead of dictating his message to them suggests that the method of personal communication was more important to him than absolute accuracy in every detail. However, I also believe that God prevented any errors that would obscure his message, since such errors would prevent it being "useful for teaching, rebuking, correcting and training in righteousness" (2 Tim 3:16).

The inspired message of the Bible does not merely concern faith and morals, as the Second Vatican Council concluded. Part of its message is that God has interacted in history, from the times of Abraham and Moses to Jesus and Paul—so historical details are also important. This means that when I come across any apparent historical contradictions, I am keen to try to solve the mystery. In fact, I revel in them, because really hard questions are often the tiny crack that opens up hidden truth. They

---

3. Mark Joseph Zia, "The Inerrancy of Scripture and the Second Vatican Council" (TinyURL.com/InerrancyVatican2).

may reveal a doorway into something the church has forgotten about—such as the importance of women's ministry in the early church. Or they may lead us to question the weak scriptural foundations for a doctrine that has been accepted for historic reasons—such as the divine right of kings.

Although God may have allowed fallible human authors to record occasional insignificant errors, this won't stop me trying to solve these apparent contradictions. Like any historian—even those investigating secular sources—I know that such problems are often due to our ignorance of details that may be explained later. Real history is always complex, and the fact that apparent problems exist demonstrates that the Bible is a collection of *real* historical documents about events when God intervened. That's the most exciting kind of history I can imagine.

8

▼

The Virgin Birth

This doctrine is rejected as mythology, even by many believers. But no Christian would invent a story that makes Jesus illegitimate! This wouldn't make him appear at all holy or special.

In our present society it is easy to forget how utterly unacceptable any slur on your parentage used to be—and in many cultures this is still the worst insult imaginable. When the Americans first tried to combat Saddam Hussein's army, they faced a seemingly insurmountable problem: they couldn't find it! The Iraqis had prepared vast warrens of underground bunkers over a huge area, and even after several weeks of bombing, the US had failed to kill or even dislodge significant numbers. Someone who knew the Iraqi culture came up with a brilliant and successful ruse. The Americans fitted loudspeakers on armored cars that were filled with snipers. They drove across the apparently empty desert broadcasting in Arabic: "Your mothers were born illegitimately." This was so unbearable for the Iraqi soldiers that they poured out of their hidden bunkers firing wildly at the loudspeakers, even though they knew they'd be easy targets for the snipers.

INSULTS ABOUT JESUS' PARENTAGE

In Nazareth, everyone knew that Jesus' conception was illegitimate, because it occurred fewer than nine months after his parents' marriage, and everyone could count. In fact, after spending three months at Elizabeth's house (Luke 1:56) and other delays, Mary probably had a visible bump on her wedding day. It would have been more socially acceptable if Joseph had been the father, but he denied this. So when Jesus had the temerity to preach at his home village, the gossiping turned into public outrage: "Isn't this the carpenter? Isn't this Mary's son and the brother of James, Joseph, Judas and Simon? Aren't his sisters here with us?" (Mark 6:3). This tirade is all the more damning because of who it leaves out—Jesus' father! It was outrageously insulting to call him "bar Mary" and then list all his family members without naming his father.

Jews in the time of Jesus took their father's name as their surname. Matthew's list of disciples includes "James son of Zebedee" and "James son of Alphaeus" (see Matt 10:2-4). In Aramaic, the Jewish language of the time, this would have been "James bar Zebedee" and "James bar Alphaeus," just like "Simon bar Jonah" (Matt 16:17). This is the pattern found in all Jewish literature of that period and, like our surnames, they kept these names even after their father had died. This sometimes caused confusion if the names were too common, in which case other surnames were used. Simon was a particularly common name, and most rabbis with this name were therefore named after their village or in other ways. There were two Simons among the twelve disciples, so one was given the nickname "Peter" (i.e., "Rocky") and the other was named "the Zealot," which may indicate his birthplace, his mood, or even his political sympathies (Matt 10:2-4). However, nowhere in the extensive volumes of ancient Jewish literature, which include several hundred names, is there any other example of a man who was named, like Jesus, after his mother. Even after someone's father had died, they continued being named after him, so Joseph's death would not explain why Jesus was called "son of Mary." This glaring omission of the name "Joseph" proclaimed the basis of the insult: no one knew who Jesus' father was.

While only Mark records this insult at Nazareth, the other Gospels couldn't ignore the charge that Jesus was illegitimate. They each respond to it in different ways, because they all have their own styles. Mark reads like a tabloid newspaper with its short sentences and immediacy. Matthew, like a serious business paper, is concerned about the political and religious establishments, and seeks to highlight corruption and hypocrisy. Luke is like a campaigning newssheet, interested in social concerns and the disadvantaged, such as lepers, women, and the poor. And the Gospel of John is like a more thoughtful weekly news magazine because it was written after a time of theological reflection and with the perspective of hindsight. But while the Gospels all have different emphases, none can ignore Jesus' illegitimacy.

Any good salesman will tell you that the best way to deal with a potential criticism is to address it head-on, and that's what Matthew and Luke did when they gave extended details about Jesus' parentage. Matthew, being concerned about the establishment, emphasized the regal star at the time of Jesus' birth, the emissaries from the East, and the malevolent interest of King Herod, who considered Jesus a possible rival. Luke also stressed that Jesus' birth was special, but concentrated on the humble shepherds and the celestial choir. In preparation for this, he started his Gospel with the genealogy of Jesus from Adam to Joseph, and then he presented the surprise: Jesus was not the son of Joseph but of the Holy Spirit. To confirm that God was behind this miracle, he depicted the piety of Mary and her relative Elizabeth, the elderly priest's wife whom Mary traveled to visit as soon as she fell pregnant. The unspoken implication is that Mary would not have confided in Elizabeth if she had anything to be ashamed of.

John is more subtle, but he couldn't ignore this well-known charge against Jesus. In this Gospel it is answered when a heckler brought it up in an attempt to disrupt Jesus' preaching. Jesus had just claimed to come from his father in heaven (John 8:18), so the heckler called out, "Where is your father?" (v. 19). When some in the crowd would have muttered, "What does he mean?," the gossips were no doubt delighted to share the juicy details. At first Jesus ignored the interruption and continued to teach about his origins from above (vv. 21-23), but when he proclaimed that those who reject him will die in their sins (v. 24) the heckler demanded: "Who are you?" (v. 25)—that is, "What's your name?" He probably hoped for an answer like "Jesus son of Joseph," so that he could dispute it, but instead, a little later, Jesus evaded this by calling himself "the Son of Man" (v. 28). Shortly after this, the heckler said: "We are Abraham's descendants" (i.e., "we are good Jews"), and Jesus retorted that if they were really Abraham's descendants, they wouldn't be trying to kill him (vv. 33-40). Now the gloves were off, and the heckler delivered an undisguised accusation: "We are not illegitimate" (v. 41)! You can almost hear the collective sharp intake of breath. Jesus answered, "You belong to your father, the devil. ... There is no truth in him. When he lies, he speaks his native language, for he is a liar and the father of lies" (v. 44). But no one was convinced by this response. They called him mad, and a blasphemer, and then tried to stone him so that he had to hide and slip away (vv. 48-59). By telling the story this way, John acknowledged that this charge was ultimately unanswerable.

This kind of slur about Jesus' birth continued for hundreds of years in rabbinic literature, where Jesus is called "son of Pandera." The origin of this tradition is unknown, but it was fairly early. It is linked to the first-century rabbi Eliezer ben Hyrcanus, the second-century Greek anti-Christian Celsus, and to Rabbi Hisda at the end of the third century. By that time, Hisda was having to explain who Pandera was, because some rabbis no longer remembered—he asserted that Pandera referred to an illicit lover.[1]

How do historians view these charges about Jesus' parentage? After his death and resurrection, the Jews were understandably skeptical about explanations in the Gospels that Jesus' father was God himself. Modern historians are equally skeptical, as they should be, because otherwise they'd be accepting the veracity of all kinds of miracles claimed for holy men of all religions throughout history. The less likely an event is, the more evidence is required to support it. However, the fact that this slur was made against Jesus by his contemporaries actually adds weight to the claimed miracle of virgin birth.

The job of historians is to question the motivation and accuracy of ancient reports and to decide, on the basis of other facts and their knowledge of human psychology, what actually happened. So, for example, when historians read Suetonius' report that several miracles and signs accompanied the birth of Emperor Augustus,[2] they have to decide whether this was over-enthusiastic hype or overt propaganda. And when they investigate the birth of Jesus, we wouldn't expect them to use different

---

1. Eliezer is at Tosefta Hullin 2:22-24 (TinyURL.com/ToseftaHul2-22); Celsus at *Contra Celsum* 1.32 (TinyURL.com/Celsus1-32), and R. Hisda at Babylonian Talmud Shabbat 104b, which was censored out of many manuscripts (TinyURL.com/JesusTalmud).

2. Suetonius, *Lives of the Caesars, Augustus* 94 (TinyURL.com/SuetAugBirth).

criteria. Historical method can never easily accept a miracle because, by any criteria of what is likely to have happened, a miracle will always be at the bottom of the list. Miracles are, by their nature, special, so they are never likely.

YOU WOULDN'T MAKE IT UP

There are significant reasons why it is also unlikely that Joseph and Mary would have invented such a strange explanation for Jesus' birth. First, they lived in a society that was relatively well educated and sophisticated, and the religious leaders of the time were particularly skeptical about improbable and unprecedented miracles. Most Jews would have regarded the story of a virgin birth as unbelievable at best and blasphemous at worst. Second, Joseph and Mary would have attracted less criticism if they'd said the child was the result of rape by a Roman soldier or due to premarital lovemaking. Conceiving a child while betrothed was viewed as unfortunate, but the child was still regarded as legitimate.[3] And if Joseph was brave enough to marry this apparently fallen woman, it makes sense that he would also have the courage to tell the truth. This story of a miraculous virgin birth was particularly dubious and, as the incidental references in the Gospels of John and Mark demonstrate, it was simply disbelieved by most Jews. They didn't believe it in his home village or in the rest of the country, and anyone who understood that society could have predicted that this story wouldn't be believed.

Historians therefore have to choose between two equally unlikely scenarios. Either a group of religious Jews adamantly proclaimed an extremely naive and potentially blasphemous story, or there really was a miraculous birth. This is an

---

3. Mishnah Qiddushin 3:12 interpreted by Tarfon in the mid-second century (TinyURL.com/MishnahQid3-12).

uncomfortable choice, except for those who do not rule out the miraculous.

For all Christians, Jesus being the brunt of gossips is a precious additional insight into his life of suffering. Isaiah predicted that the Messiah would be despised and rejected, sorrowful and grieving, afflicted with illness, wounds, and punishments so severe that people would assume that he was being stricken by God (Isa 53:3–5). The question of his parentage was a scandal he bore alongside all those who are falsely branded with moral disapproval for something outside their control—for example, those who don't know their parents, rape victims, and those who suffer moral stigma as a result of child abuse or homosexual inclinations. Jesus' illegitimacy is a further demonstration that when God became human, he shared all our suffering and every aspect of our fallen humanity so that he could represent and redeem everyone.

9

▼

Church Divisions

A split occurred in Acts 6 that eventually divided Paul's churches from Jewish congregations. Paul found a way to minimize the damage. Can we learn from this how to heal our own divisions?

My friend Ken showed me a strange photo of the two small Baptist churches for which he was the joint minister in a South Wales village. The churches were next to each other, and in the photo the two congregations stand on the steps leading up to each of their front doors, with Ken standing astride a small dividing wall with a foot on each set of steps. They shared him as their minister because neither church could pay his salary by themselves. When he took on the dual pastorate, he assumed that he'd be able to unite the churches into one, but they absolutely refused. Despite his urging, even though they believed the same things, heard the same sermons from him, had occasional joint services, and shared friendships, they were determined they wouldn't amalgamate. Why? One church worshiped in English and one in Welsh.

Jews in Jerusalem during New Testament times were split in a similar way. Most of them were locals who spoke Aramaic, but many pious Greek-speaking Jews from other countries retired there to be closer to the Temple. The two groups worshiped in separate synagogues, using different translations of Scripture.

Both synagogues revered the Bible in Hebrew, but in one it was translated into Greek, and in the other it was translated into Aramaic—a language descended from Hebrew in a similar way that Italian descended from Latin. So the synagogues reflected a deep division in society.

SQUABBLING WIDOWS

The first Christian church in Jerusalem faced the same problem, especially when a large number of Greek-speaking foreigners were converted at Pentecost. However, the church was determined to remain together in a single, mixed community (Acts 2:44). Before too long, though, a split started during an apparently minor dispute. A group of widows whom the church fed at communal meals started bickering about favoritism. Some Greek-speaking widows complained that the deacons (Greek for "servants," or in this case, "waiters") were giving them smaller portions than the Aramaic-speaking widows. The disciples addressed this problem by appointing Greek-speaking leaders to the team (Acts 6:1–6). This halted the immediate crisis, but it was the start of a split that became a permanent divide.

A surprising outcome of this first split was its effect on evangelism, because some of the newly appointed Greek leaders (including Philip and Stephen) became powerful evangelists. The Jewish leaders reacted violently, and following Stephen's martyrdom, the Greek-speaking Christians fled abroad to avoid persecution. This resulted in evangelism in many more cities, but also divided the church geographically.

One of the main persecutors of these Greek believers was Saul, who was converted while pursuing them. Using his Greek name, Paul, he became the greatest evangelist to the Greek-speaking world—and found himself effectively the head of a rival church. The believers in Jerusalem continued worshiping alongside Jews in the Temple, but Paul's increasingly Gentile church was gradually regarded as a separate religion. The schism became permanent, though the Jewish Christian groups (later called Nazarenes and Ebionites) only lasted a couple of centuries before dying out.

Paul went to great lengths to try healing this rift by collecting money for the impoverished Jerusalem church and working with them to dispel myths about his anti-Jewish bias (1 Cor 16:1). Ultimately, though, he failed. His plan was to be publicly seen sponsoring some men who were making a vow offering in the Temple. But this went disastrously wrong when some Jews in the Temple thought that Paul's friends were Gentiles whom Paul had sneaked into the inner court. In the ensuing riot, Paul was arrested by Roman soldiers, and Jewish leaders charged him with destroying the harmony brought by (or imposed by) the Romans (Acts 24:1–21).

Similar schisms were probably happening in John's community when he wrote his Gospel. Synagogues rejected early Christians as heretical because they were proclaiming that Jesus was the Messiah. Also, sadly, judging from the way John emphasized Jesus' pleas for unity, there were also divisions among these believers. John records that after his final meal with the disciples, Jesus prayed for his church: "that all of them may be one ... so that they may be brought to complete unity. Then the world will know that you sent me and have loved them even as you have loved me" (John 17:21, 23).

These splits would have discredited the gospel in Greco-Roman society, where harmony was one of the greatest virtues. Dissension among the members of any group was regarded as a serious vice. The Romans strove to create unity in the empire by respecting all religions and even by building expensive temples for the gods of conquered people. Even when addressing the emperor, you could get away with telling him that he should seek a more harmonious relationship with his conquered enemies.[1]

Many of the most eloquent and memorable passages in the New Testament were written to combat rivalry and disharmony. This theme is clear in the carefully constructed "One Lord, one faith" passage in Ephesians 4, and the elegant, image-filled passage about controlling the tongue in James 3. Even the beautiful poem about love in 1 Corinthians 13 is a call for unity, placed between two chapters concerning the particularly divisive subjects of worship styles and spiritual gifts. Perhaps this is one reason why it is so appropriate at weddings!

On the whole, it seems that the early church took the need for unity to heart—in the first two centuries, new believers were attracted to the church, saying, "See how they love one another." Church leader Tertullian recorded this comment in the third century,[2] but by the next century everything changed. Soon after Constantine proclaimed Christianity as the official religion in AD 312, Christians started to publicly curse each other with anathemas.

An anathema, meaning "accursed," was a public proclamation of excommunication, and it gradually became a weapon of church politics. The first anathema was proclaimed at the Council of Elvira (AD 306) against serious sexual offenders, which was certainly a good reason to exclude them. Then in AD 340 the Synod of Gangra anathematized those who were ascetic for the wrong motives—that is, for self-aggrandizement instead of self-abasement. Gradually this method was used more commonly to condemn differences in theology than to condemn

---

1. This happens twice in the senatorial *Speech to Caesar* 5.3; 6.5 (TinyURL.com/SallustCaesar).

2. *Apologeticus pro Christianis* 39 (TinyURL.com/Tertullian-love).

sinful lifestyles. At the Council of Ephesus (AD 431), for example, Cyril of Alexandria passed anathemas against Nestorius for calling Mary the Mother of Christ instead of Mother of God. Nestorius' followers retaliated by forming their own synod, at which they denounced Cyril. Such conduct, often over minor differences, has continued to split the church, until we now have over thirty-four thousand denominations.

DEADLY DIVISIONS

The Jewish world at the time of Jesus was like the modern church—divided into countless factions—and this weakness almost destroyed it. The community that preserved the Dead Sea Scrolls was separated from other Jews by a different religious calendar—just like the Catholic and Orthodox split was exacerbated by different dates for Christmas and Easter. Sadducees and Pharisees were split by theological issues such as the afterlife and angels (which Sadducees rejected), similar to the doctrines that divide modern liberal and conservative theologians. And the Pharisees, like modern Protestants, were divided into countless smaller groups. Almost all we know about the two most famous Pharisee groups is found in a long ancient catalogue of their 316 disagreements, often about very minor matters!

Jesus, paradoxically, managed to unite the Pharisees and Sadducees when they had to cooperate to accuse him before the Romans. They couldn't repeat this rare moment of unity when they attempted to accuse Paul before the Romans, because Paul exploited their differences. He provoked them into an open argument with each other in the courtroom until the trial ended with a riot (Acts 23:1–10).

The splits within Judaism almost destroyed it. When the Zealots (Jewish terrorists) took over Jerusalem, causing the Romans to attack the city, the Pharisees and Sadducees failed to unite to stop this disaster. In AD 70, the Romans destroyed the city and Temple, and almost every Jewish leader was massacred. The few who survived decided to do things differently from that time on: they agreed to discuss all issues and abide by majority decisions after a public vote. Following this principle, a new, united Judaism was born.

Judaism learned some hard lessons about unity—and how to work toward it—at a time of weakness. Churches sometimes learn the same lesson when they are in the minority or persecuted. When there are fewer of us, our differences seem less important than the Savior whom we have in common. But when churches grow strong, it becomes easier to split and to disobey the only specifically new commandment Jesus gave us: "Love one another" (John 13:34).

The same tribal instincts that divide people into street gangs and social cliques make Christians exaggerate small differences and create new denominations. Our emphasis, however, should be on the things that unite us. In Paul's letter to the Philippians—written when two of its members, Euodia and Syntyche, were embattled (Phil 4:2)—he makes his famous plea to think about what is honorable, pure, and praiseworthy (Phil 4:8). Instead of highlighting our rivals' failings and vices, let's take Paul's words to heart and look for "whatever is true, whatever is noble, whatever is right, whatever is pure, whatever is lovely, and whatever is admirable" *in them*, because this will lead us all to the peace of God.

Section 2

▾

Doctrines That Confuse

10

▼

Prooftexts

Flat-earthers, Christian Scientists, and others support their view-points from the Bible but make errors in how they do this. We can avoid similar common mistakes in reasoning.

Can the Bible be made to say whatever you want? You might well think so when you see Christians arguing polar-opposite points from the Bible text, or appearing to make the Bible say strange things. However, when we look closely, we can see that errors in biblical interpretation usually happen because of common mistakes in reasoning.

For example, Cosmas Indicopleustes, a sixth-century monk, traveled widely and wrote a long book called *Christian Topography*, with wonderful maps and illustrations. He wanted to prove that the pagans were wrong to teach that the earth was a sphere, and he used the Bible to prove that the earth is flat—along with many arguments citing "obvious" facts.[1] He often referred to Isaiah 40:22, which describes the world as a "circle" (Hebrew *khug*). He has a point, because this word is related to *mekhugah*, "compass," an item that is used for drawing a circle on a flat surface (Isa 44:13), when instead Isaiah could have used the word *kaddur*, meaning a "sphere" or "ball," as used in Isaiah

---

1. See the full text at TinyURL.com/Cosmas-Indico.

22:18. However, Cosmas was nevertheless mistaken to use this verse to conclude the earth is flat—and it would be just as wrong to conclude from it that the earth is a sphere. Isaiah shouldn't be used to prove either, because this ignores the context of the verse and applies it contrary to the purpose of the text, which is to glorify God and not to teach astronomy. In this way, ignoring the context of the text when we read it can lead to wrong interpretations.

A second example of a common mistake in interpreting the Bible comes from Christian Scientists, who argue that we can defeat illness when we realize that it is not real but merely part of the "dream" that we live in. They find this dream revealed in Genesis 2:21, which says that God put Adam to sleep but doesn't say that he woke up—the implication being that we are all part of Adam's dream.[2] Their interpretation isn't quite as simplistic as this summary suggests, but it is nevertheless mistaken because they base their argument on silence. That is, they came to a conclusion based on something the text doesn't say and where the silence isn't particularly surprising. It is true that some silences in the Bible are significant, such as the lack of any mention or even a hint that Jesus ever sinned. But most silences are insignificant because we shouldn't expect everything to be spelled out. For example, the Gospels never mention that Jesus ever went to the toilet. This silence led some early church fathers to conclude that he had a different kind of digestion so he never had to do anything so undivine![3] So the argument from silence can occasionally be valid, but it should be applied with caution.

---

2. An official article on this doctrine is L. Ivimy Gwalter, "The Truth of Being versus the Dream" (TinyURL.com/CSJ-Dream).

3. Clement, *Stromata* 7.59 (TinyURL.com/ClemStrom7-59).

The ancient rabbis made a third common mistake: they mixed up generalized and particular statements. God told humanity in general to "be fruitful and increase in number" (Gen 1:28), but the rabbis regarded this as a command for every individual to seek to get married and have children. They concluded that every couple had to have at least two children—either two boys (like Moses) or a boy and a girl (like God did)—yes, they really did reason in that way![4] We often make a similar though opposite error with regard to promises in the Bible, such as God's assurance to Abraham that "I am your shield; your reward shall be very great." Although we can learn about the general character of God from this—that he looks out for his people—this doesn't mean that each of us will be protected and enriched just like God promised to Abraham. We shouldn't generalize from a particular instance or apply a general statement to every individual.

THE WEAKEST LINK

Mistakes in biblical interpretation are sometimes silly and easily avoided, but they can also have serious consequences when it comes to undermining the trustworthiness of the Bible. If you try to persuade someone to a particular viewpoint by a series of arguments, they will pick on the weakest one to argue against it. If they can show that it falls flat, they will conclude (probably wrongly) that your whole case is flawed. This isn't a logical conclusion, but it is the way our minds work, and we all tend to do it unless we guard strongly against it. It is part of the reason why so many people reject the Bible. Because they have heard its text being used in a faulty way to prove something silly, they wrongly conclude that the Bible can't be trusted or that it's just foolish.

---

4. See the debate at Tosefta Yebamot 8.4 (TinyURL.com/TophYeb8-4).

For example, the modern homosexuality debate has produced rather a lot of misuses of Scripture. This is probably because the debate is so heated, and people are largely speaking to their own supporters rather than actually trying to engage with the other side. Interpreters from one extreme want to remove any mention of homosexuality from the Bible, so they argue that we can't know what the Greek word *arsenokoitēs* means. It is true that the word occurs only twice (1 Cor 6:9 and 1 Tim 1:10) and that it occurs nowhere outside the Bible—except in later comments about these passages. However, it is clear that it is a combination of two words: *arsēn* and *koitē*, which mean "man" and "bed," respectively. And it is fairly obvious that they are combined in this way because they follow each other in the ancient Greek translation of Leviticus 20:13: "If a man beds a male [*arsenos koitēn*] ..." (my translation). Since this combination of words occurs nowhere else, no reader in the first century would have failed to see that link with the prohibition in Leviticus.

Some argue, from the other side, that "God made Adam and Eve, not Adam and Steve." This argument falls down as soon as you imagine the opposite. If God *had* made Adam and Steve, the first pair of humans would have been the last, because they couldn't have had children. Logically, therefore, the first couple *had* to be a mixed-sex couple. Even if God wanted 50 percent of the couples in Genesis to be same-sex (instead of the 0 percent we find there), he would still have had to make the first couple male and female. "Not Adam and Steve" makes a catchy slogan, but it is poor exegesis.

Argument from silence is also used in this debate when people say that prohibitions of homosexuality don't refer to long-term committed relationships because these aren't mentioned in the Bible. However, arguments from silence only work when one would overwhelmingly expect something to be said. For example, the law that says you cannot marry your wife's sister includes the words "while your wife is living" (Lev 18:18). Without those words, it would be clear that you could never marry your wife's sister, just as you can never marry your mother. Similarly, the law about men sleeping together *could* have included the words "unless they are committed to each other," but without a phrase like this, it clearly includes all men. One can't argue that the silence with regard to long-term commitment means that this is excluded.

JESUS' WISDOM

Jesus used the Bible in a responsible way, without ignoring the context, arguing from silence, or applying particulars as generalizations. In a debate about divorce, he quoted, "For this reason a man will leave his father and mother and be united to his wife, and the two will become one flesh" (Matt 19:5, citing Gen 2:24). The verse he cited from Genesis is about humans in general and not only about Adam and Eve, so he wasn't generalizing from a particular. Furthermore, its original purpose was to teach what marriage was like, so he wasn't applying it contrary to this. He emphasized the central point of the text: that couples should become one and remain united.

Jesus also didn't misuse this general text by making it apply to every individual couple in particular. Some marriages do become broken when one partner breaks their vows, and Jesus allowed for divorce in such cases. He used this text to argue that divorce *shouldn't* happen, but he didn't use it to show that divorce *cannot* happen when one partner does repeatedly break their vows.

And Jesus didn't misuse the text by emphasizing an inconsequential detail, such as forbidding couples from living in a parental home on the basis that the text says that they "leave" their parents. This isn't the intended purpose of the text, so we shouldn't create a command out of a detail that just happens to be mentioned.

Returning to the modern homosexuality debate, people make this error when they argue that this verse defines marriage as a man plus a woman. Clearly this is the *assumption* behind the text, because it doesn't say "when two people," but it isn't the *purpose* of the text. Genesis 2:24 is concerned with the strength and closeness of marriage, not its sexual makeup. This text *could* have excluded homosexual marriages by (for example) following the words "united to his wife" with "but not to a man." Or (just to be fair), Genesis *could* have promoted homosexual marriages by adding "or his husband." But it did neither. So the text shouldn't be used as proof one way or the other.

I cringe when I hear the two sides of this debate using these "proofs" for their case. The problem with using prooftexts in this way is that we debase the whole Bible. It is also a poor way to argue, because when people see through our weak argument, they are likely to throw out everything else we say. But even worse, they may reject the Bible itself because of us. Even when our conclusion is correct, it is counterproductive and damaging to base it on irrelevant or misleading texts. If we really want to take the Bible seriously, we should take extra care not to misuse it. With Bible interpretation, as with most things, the ends don't justify the means.

11

▼

Acts of God

In the Bible, the prophets predicted disasters and used them as warnings from God. Should we regard all disasters as retribution from God? This traditional church doctrine is rarely heard today—for good reasons.

When Benjamin Franklin invented the lightning rod in 1752, the pope recommended it, but many churches refused to install one. They believed that it interfered with God's sovereign right to strike down sinners. Instead, they continued with the practice of ringing the church bells during lightning storms to call people to pray and to ward off the lightning. Unfortunately this resulted in many bell ringers being killed by lightning—an average of three a year in Germany (where, for some reason, they kept a count). Things didn't change until 1769, when the church of Saint Nazaire in Brescia, Italy, was struck by lightning. This ignited the gunpowder stored in its large underground vaults—about one hundred tons! The explosion killed three thousand people and destroyed a sixth of the town. After this, most churches quickly fitted lighting rods to their spires.[1]

---

1. See Vladimir A. Rakov and Martin A. Uman, *Lightning: Physics and Effects* (Cambridge: Cambridge University Press, 2003), 2–3.

The concept of an "act of God" started with the Laws of Hammurabi, a Babylonian law code from about 3,800 years ago. Law 249 stated that if a man hired an ox and a god struck it with lightning, he did not have to pay compensation. Today, only insurance brokers refer to lightning as an "act of God," although when lightning caused a serious fire at York Minster in 1984, many people related it to the service held there to consecrate David Jenkins as the new bishop of Durham three days earlier. Some newspapers had reported that this bishop didn't believe in the resurrection. Was God agreeing with them and making his feelings known in this way?

PLAGUES AND AIDS

In previous centuries, the doctrine of divine retribution—that God punishes society's evils through natural disasters such as famines and plagues—was accepted by all Christians. J. C. Ryle (1816–1900), Anglican bishop of Liverpool, was a famous advocate. He interpreted the eighteenth-century cholera outbreak in London as a result of "sabbath breaking, drunkenness, infidelity, blasphemy, fornication."[2] And he regarded insanitary conditions as merely a secondary cause—the primary cause was God himself. The doctrine of divine retribution is still occasionally invoked—such as when the AIDS epidemic first affected mostly homosexual men—but it is rarely taken seriously anymore. This means that there is no easy theological response when huge disasters occur, such as the Indian Ocean tsunami of 2004, which resulted in 230,000 deaths and 1.7 million homeless (mostly Muslims), or the Haitian earthquake of 2010, which left 316,000 people dead and 1.6 million homeless

---

2. J. C. Ryle, *"The Hand of the Lord!" Being Thoughts on Cholera* (London: William Hunt, 1865), 10.

(mostly Christians). Every year we see more disasters on our increasing number of news channels and, as we watch the suffering of so many, the question stays the same: Why?

Should we ascribe the killing of apparently innocent people to God when a natural disaster occurs? Jesus was presented with this question when he was asked about the collapse of a tower in Siloam, which had recently killed eighteen people, and the killing of innocent bystanders by soldiers in the Temple (Luke 13:1–5). Although the second example wasn't exactly natural, it was outside the control of ordinary people, so it felt the same. The victims of both incidents didn't appear to have done anything especially wrong, so why did God let them die this way? Did they have secret sins that God was punishing? As we'll see, Jesus regarded these as undeserved disasters, but God nevertheless used them for his purposes.

Old Testament stories such as the destruction of Sodom or the earthquake in King Uzziah's day suggest that God does sometimes use earthly disasters as punishment. But were these disasters initiated by him in order to do his will, or were they going to happen anyway and God *used* them to carry out his will? The Bible accounts suggest the second option: God makes use of natural disasters that would happen anyway; he doesn't initiate them in order to punish us.

Sodom's destruction is portrayed in the Bible as a natural disaster that God used as a punishment. When he spoke to Abraham about what was going to happen, he said that he would save everyone in the city if enough of them were righteous. Although we are not told how they would be saved, presumably it would be the same way as Lot—by evacuation. God isn't pictured as having his hand on the button, waiting until Lot is safe before he presses it. Instead, the urgency of the angels who dragged Lot's family out of the city implies that they had no control, which suggests that God was using a disaster rather than initiating it specially (Gen 19:15–17). It was a natural event that was going to happen whether the angels were ready or not, and they knew that God wasn't planning to stop it. However, God was able to use it as a punishment by only rescuing the righteous.

When an earthquake shook the kingdoms of Israel and Judah in about 760 BC, the fact that Amos had prophesied about God's judgment just two years previously made people assume that God had deliberately chosen to send it. But there are good reasons to doubt this. The ruler of the southern kingdom of Judah, Uzziah (aka Azariah), was generally good (though he did bad things later, after the quake), and his people were no worse than previous generations (2 Kgs 15:3–4). And although Israel's king, Jeroboam, is described as "bad," in fact all Israel's kings are labeled in that way. Actually, Jeroboam was better than most because he followed God's guidance to rescue the people (2 Kgs 14:26–27). However, during these reigns there was a new evil, which Amos highlights: many people got wealthy at the expense of the poor. The wise foreign policies of these kings had made a lot of people rich (see 2 Chr 26:8–10; 2 Kgs 14:25), but as Amos complained, they didn't care about those who remained poor (Amos 2:6–8). Perhaps that's why Amos specified that their fine, strong mansions would be destroyed—though this was by fire and enemies, not by an earthquake (2:5; 3:11, 15). We should assume that, when the earthquake came, the houses of the poor and rich alike were destroyed.

Amos concluded: "When disaster comes to a city, has not the Lord caused it?" (Amos 3:6). He was reminding the people that everything comes from God—bad things as well as good things (which is how his prophecy ends, at 9:11–15). When bad things happen, we should listen to what God might be saying. Of course, God wants all generations to listen to him, but this particular generation had a special opportunity to hear him clearly. In giving Amos this prophecy shortly before a natural disaster occurred, God got their complete attention by showing his foreknowledge. He used this event to present his timeless message in a way that would be remembered and acted on. Amos' generation wasn't worse than others, but it received and listened to a warning we should all heed.

UNLESS YOU REPENT

Jesus gave a similar message when he was asked about the disasters in his day. His conclusion was that those who suffered weren't worse sinners than the others, but their suffering acted as a warning to all: "Unless *you* repent, *you* too will all perish" (Luke 13:3). This is not exactly a comforting message to hear! So what was Jesus' message about the innocent who suffer? In effect, it was that there aren't any innocent people because we are all sinners. Actually, Jesus didn't quite say that no one is innocent of sin, because he said "Unless you repent, you too will all perish." He didn't say "we," like any other preacher would, which implies that he didn't count himself among sinners deserving to perish—but he is the only exception.

Jesus was pointing out that these disasters can be considered minor compared to the judgment that will come to everyone. He didn't acknowledge any surprise that people were killed in these disasters, because in a wicked and fallen world we should expect this kind of thing to happen. This is not the good and perfect world that God was planning for humanity before sin infected it. Jesus implied that the surprising thing is that we sinners should experience *any good* in this world.

Jesus taught that we are all evil, and yet God nevertheless loves us. He warned that our occasional goodness doesn't nullify our underlying evil nature. He said: "You don't give a stone to your children when they ask for bread, even though you are evil" (Matt 7:9-11). In other words: "You might do good things, but you are still sinful." Another time, when someone politely called him "good rabbi," he reminded them that only God can really be called "good." He didn't want anyone to forget that compared to God, we are all fundamentally evil. We all need God's forgiveness, even if we do good things a lot of the time. Despite this, Jesus proclaimed God's forgiveness (Mark 2:5-11), saying that God is longing to do good for us even more than we are longing to do good for our own children (Matt 7:9-11).

The mystery of natural disasters is not that God allows evil to happen to good people. Jesus' message implies the real mystery of suffering is that there is so little of it. We experience so much undeserved good that we complain when things go wrong. In our fallen world there will always be disasters, and relatively good people will suffer alongside relatively bad people. But those who listen to Jesus will find a salutary reminder in those disasters. It is a reminder that a real judgment is coming that will be totally just and that God offers an eternity without disasters for those who turn to him in repentance.

12

▾

Remarriage

The New Testament hardly mentions remarriage, so how can we know what it teaches about this? The key lies in Jewish and Roman regulations, which assumed that most people would remarry. The relative silence in the New Testament is therefore very significant!

When Linda and Glynn Wolfe married, they held the world record for remarriage—for Linda it was her twenty-third wedding, and it was Glynn's twenty-ninth. It ended with his death a year later in 1997. His son John said that his father married so many times because he was a Baptist minister and didn't believe in "living in sin," but he was very picky and stubborn so the marriages didn't last long. Linda reportedly started looking for another husband after Glynn died.[1]

The Roman world of New Testament days was familiar with multiple remarriages. Seneca complained (in about AD 60) that "there are women who number the years ... by their husbands; they divorce to marry and they marry to divorce."[2] Paradoxically, we can blame the morality campaign of the Emperor Augustus just before Jesus was born. He was concerned that too few legitimate citizens were being born, so he made it illegal to delay

---

1. See "Glynn Wolfe," *Wikipedia* (TinyURL.com/GlynnWolfe).
2. *De beneficiis* book 3, section 16 (TinyURL.com/SenecaMarriage).

remarriage. Anyone who didn't remarry within two years of being widowed or within eighteen months of being divorced could suffer financial penalties.[3]

The Jewish world had similar ideas, though for different reasons. Jews regarded it as impious to remain single because the first command in the Bible is "be fruitful and increase in number" (Gen 1:28). If your marriage ended without a minimum of two children, you were expected to remarry. Rabbi Simeon ben Azzai was badgered by his fellow rabbis because he wouldn't remarry. Eventually they stopped when he said, "I am married—to the Scriptures." But normal Jews didn't have this excuse.[4]

REQUIRED BY LAW

Both Roman and Jewish societies expected anyone who was divorced or widowed to remarry. This was even expected of older widows, who were expected to marry for both financial and emotional support. The example of Anna, who spent her life in worship after being widowed, was highlighted as remarkable both because of her piety and because she remained single (Luke 2:36-37). Paul urged younger widows in Timothy's church to get remarried because single widows might be tempted into sexual immorality or spend their time in idle gossip (1 Tim 5:11-14).

What about divorcées in the church—could they remarry? On the face of it, the answer is no, for four reasons:

1. Jesus said that people who remarried were committing adultery (Matt 19:9).

2. Paul said a divorcée should not remarry (1 Cor 7:11).

---

3. The *lex Iulia et Papia* (TinyURL.com/LexJuliaEtPapia).
4. Tosefta Yebamot 8.4 (TinyURL.com/TophYeb8-4).

3. Married people are "one flesh," which sounds permanent (Matt 19:5).

4. Paul said that marriage can only end with death, not divorce (1 Cor 7:39; Rom 7:2).

A list like this sounds convincing, but each of these reasons is based on misunderstandings.

First, Jesus' teaching concerned the newly invented "any cause" type of divorce. He said this was nonbiblical and invalid, so that any remarriage after this was adultery because the first marriage hadn't actually ended.[5] But this doesn't mean that Jesus regarded biblical divorces as similarly invalid.

Second, the divorcée whom Paul told not to remarry was one who had divorced without any biblical grounds. She was told not to remarry because she should seek reconciliation. However, if her ex-husband refused reconciliation, this reason for forbidding remarriage no longer applied. In the same chapter, Paul told other deserted believers that they were "not bound" (1 Cor 7:15). First-century readers would have recognized his unusual use of "bound" (which was normally only used concerning slaves), though Jews often used this concept with regard to a divorce certificate.[6] They would have realized that Paul was saying that this person was free to remarry—and therefore that he allowed remarriage after a divorce based on biblical grounds such as abandonment.

Third, the phrase "one flesh" does sound permanent—and it is supposed to. It emphasizes that sexual union involves the whole person, and that's why it should be reserved for marriage. Paul uses the same concept when persuading people to desist

---

5. See more details in my books at www.DivorceRemarriage.com.
6. As in the discussion at Mishnah Gittin 9:3 (TinyURL.com/MishnahGit9-3).

from becoming "one flesh" with prostitutes (1 Cor 6:16). He is using this phrase to show that a sexual union *should* be permanent, but sin can stop it being so. If Paul thought that a "one flesh" relationship with a prostitute was unbreakably permanent, he'd have to tell virtually every male Roman convert to avoid marriage, because they had already become "one flesh" with the first women they slept with.

Finally, 1 Corinthians 7:39 and Romans 7:2 do say that marriage ends with death, but they don't rule out divorce as a way of ending a marriage. Neither verse mentions divorce, because this wouldn't fit the context. The first is addressed to widows, so we wouldn't expect it to say anything about divorce (1 Cor 7:39-40), and the second concerns a spiritual marriage to the "law" or "Christ," so divorce doesn't fit into this context either. Paul reasons that Jews are like someone married to the law, and they can't marry Christ except by death—which ends their marriage. In this extended metaphor, he says that Christ's death (which we share) can end their marriage to the law. If Paul tried to include divorce, it would stretch this metaphor to the breaking point.

NO EXPLICIT COMMAND

Therefore, at first glance the New Testament does appear to forbid remarriage, but on further investigation it is actually very quiet on the subject. It doesn't explicitly forbid remarriage, but nor is there any clear permission or encouragement. This is surprising, because we'd expect there to be clear teaching on such an important issue. The most likely reason for this absence is that there was no need to teach Jewish or Gentile converts about this, because Christian teaching didn't oppose what they already knew. Roman law penalized those who didn't remarry, and Jewish religious law regarded you as impious if you didn't remarry. So both societies assumed that you would remarry, and without specific teaching, Christians would assume they were allowed to. If Jesus or Paul had wanted to oppose this general assumption, they'd have to say so very clearly, but they weren't opposed to it, so they didn't need to say anything. It would be like telling believers they were allowed to pay taxes.

Unfortunately, later church fathers taught very differently because they had lost touch with the social roots of Jewish beliefs. By the second century, Christians were distancing themselves from the increasingly immoral and sexually corrupt Roman society, so they started to read the New Testament differently—without the social background of the first Christians. As a result, they thought there were four reasons against remarriage (as listed above), just as modern readers do.

Actually, although Paul didn't specifically write about remarriage after divorce, by a convoluted process we can uncover what he *thought* about it. In 1 Corinthians 7:39 he quoted the last sentence of a standard Jewish divorce certificate: "You are now free to marry anyone you wish." Paul quoted this in relation to widows, not divorcées, so he wasn't using it to state anything about divorce. He quoted this divorce certificate because Jewish law obliged childless widows to marry their brother-in-law in order to produce an heir, and he wanted to rescue them from this obligation. By quoting the divorce certificate, he invited his readers to reason: if a divorced person can marry whomever they wish, then surely a widow (who is often more vulnerable) should also be allowed this right. This reasoning is sound, and is a wonderful release for widows who might otherwise have to marry someone they didn't like. For our inquiry, it is significant that this reasoning *assumes* that a divorcée can remarry. In other words, Paul never bothered to *state* that a divorcée can remarry (because there was no need for him to do this), but he did *assume* it. Also, he knew that his reasoning would only work if his fellow believers also assumed that remarriage was allowed.

This long, convoluted, and complicated process of reasoning has finally brought us to what Jesus and Paul regarded as too obvious to state clearly: that someone with a valid divorce is free to remarry. It's like a study into dental care that takes years and costs the earth to show what most people would regard as obvious: that poorer people spend less on dental care than others. This may well be obvious, but it is also valuable for justifying policy in that area. And for someone who is divorced, the knowledge that remarriage is permitted is worth the extended brainwork necessary to get this simple answer.

13

▼

Original Sin

Augustine taught that babies inherit Adam's guilt even before they sin—but this was based on a faulty Latin translation of Romans 5:12. So does that mean we aren't born sinful?

I love the playful rhyming in Tom Lehrer's "Vatican Rag": "Take your place in the processional / Step into that small confessional / There, the guy who's got religion'll / Tell you if your sin's original." Catholic priests really have heard it all before because sin is boringly repetitive and unoriginal! But why is that? Is sin in our genes? Are all our sins rooted in an original sin committed by Adam?

The doctrine of original sin was promulgated by Augustine (AD 354–430), who taught that we inherit guilt from Adam via our parents. He didn't just say that we were born with a sinful urge (which everyone agrees with), but that we are already sinners when we are born, before we have had a chance to sin by ourselves, because we inherit the guilt of Adam's sin. It is easy to confuse the doctrine of original sin with that of original sinfulness—that is, the teaching that all humans are born with the inclination and natural propensity to sin, so that all humans are sinners because they all sin. Therefore, in order to save confusion, I'm going to refer to Augustine's doctrine as the doctrine of "original guilt."[1]

ADAM'S SIN

Part of Augustine's reasoning depended on the rather laughable idea that Adam's sin is transferred during sexual intercourse! This was the only way he could explain why Jesus didn't inherit Adam's guilt. Augustine regarded sex as inherently sinful, perhaps because of his rather misspent youth—a time during which he uttered his famous prayer, "Grant me chastity and continence, but not yet."[2] However, the five million babies conceived by in vitro fertilization during the last three decades have proved him wrong in that detail. They sin just like those conceived in the traditional way! So was Augustine also wrong about the rest of the doctrine of original guilt?

He developed this doctrine in order to combat a heresy.[3] Pelagius, a theologian whom Augustine was combatting, believed that humans could be sinless because Jesus referred to Abel as "righteous" (Matt 23:35), which implied he'd been killed before committing any sin. Augustine countered that Abel might not have sinned personally, but he was still guilty, because even newborn babies have guilt. To prove this he quoted Romans 5:12 from his Latin translation of the New Testament: "Sin entered the world through one man, and death through sin, and in this way death came to all people, *in whom* all sinned." Augustine interpreted the rather odd phrase "in whom all sinned" to mean "in

---

1. For more details see Jesse Couenhoven, "St. Augustine's Doctrine of Original Sin," *Augustinian Studies* 36 (2005), at TinyURL.com/AugustineOriginalSin.

2. Augustine, *Confessions* 8.7.17 (TinyURL.com/AugustineChastity).

3. Augustine, *On Nature and Grace* 11 (TinyURL.com/AugNatureGrace).

Adam all sinned," so that literally, when Adam sinned, every human born from him shared that guilt.[4]

But Augustine's proof was based on a faulty translation from the original Greek into Latin. The Greek verse has *eph hō* ("because," Latin *quia*), but if this was changed just a little to *en hō* it could be understood as "in whom" (Latin *in quo*). No Greek manuscripts say *en hō*, so it looks as if the Latin translator read it wrongly. The meaning of this verse (as found in all translations made from the Greek) is actually "death came to all people, because all sinned." That is, humans don't inherit guilt from Adam, but all humans personally sin, and thereby become guilty.

Before we glibly discard Augustine's doctrine of original guilt, though, we'd better consider what we would be losing. We may need some concept of original guilt in order to explain Jesus' uniqueness and why he had to die for all. After all, if we are born without any inherited guilt, it might be remotely possible for some people to get through life without sinning—which would mean Jesus didn't need to die for them. However, I can't see that this is possible. Having brought up two children, I know how soon the propensity to sin reveals itself, and I can't believe that anyone would get even to toddler stage without having done something wrong.

On the other hand, the advantage in rejecting the doctrine is that we don't have to worry that innocent babies go to hell. If people aren't born guilty, God will judge us for our actual sins and not merely for being born human. We must not underestimate the seriousness of sin. Sin is refusing to do what God wants. The actions themselves may have huge consequences

---

4. Augustine, *Against Two Letters of the Pelagians* 4.7 (TinyURL.com/AugustinePelagius).

for other people, but perhaps the greatest consequence comes from the fact that we have disobeyed God.

Animals exhibit similar tendencies to the human traits of greed, lust, cruelty, and deceit, and we can often see those faults even in our pets! Animal studies have found tribal warfare among chimps, along with rape, killing, and even eating of enemies. Sadly, one study of motherhood among dolphins came to an abrupt halt when an aunt stole a baby dolphin and thwarted all attempts to reunite it with its true mother. But the fact that these behaviors are similar to human sins does not mean that they *are* sins.

COULD DO BETTER

As James 4:17 puts it, "If anyone, then, knows the good they ought to do and doesn't do it, it is sin for them." These acts by animals aren't sins because they have no knowledge of what they should or shouldn't do. Our animal instincts became sins when God called Adam to a higher lifestyle. God gave us a conscience, which increasingly guides us as we mature, so that even without God's written law humans have a knowledge of right and wrong. This law tells us to live differently from animals: we should not mate with whoever happens to be available; we should not snatch food or other things that belong to others; and we should not kill those who challenge us.

So when we do sin, it is a personal effrontery to God, who has asked us not to follow these animal instincts. Psalm 51 shows that David realized he had offended God when he slept with Bathsheba and had her husband killed (2 Sam 11:2–14). These crimes had victims, from whom David needed to ask forgiveness, but David knew he also needed to ask God to forgive him. God had treated David as special—he had given him the Holy Spirit to help him resist temptation (Ps 51:11). David knew that without the Holy Spirit he would follow the evil inclinations he'd felt from birth (v. 5), so he asked God to cleanse him again and create a new heart in him (vv. 7–10).

In the New Testament, David's special treatment became normal for all Christians. The Holy Spirit creates a new heart in everyone who repents, and Paul said that the Spirit gives Christians the ability to conquer sin (Rom 8:3–6). Yet most of us are gross underachievers in this regard.

Perhaps the doctrine of original guilt removes some of our motivation to conquer sin, because being born with guilt makes us feel it isn't worth trying to overcome it. We regard ourselves as hopeless sinners, so there's little point in trying to be different. We feel that God is displeased with us anyway, and because his judgment is dealt with by his Son, we don't worry too much.

Perhaps we would respond differently if, instead of concentrating on God's judgment, we concentrate instead on his love for us. This may make us more aware of his disappointment when we fail to live up to the wonderful new human nature he has given us in Jesus. Perhaps we would be heartbroken (as God is) when we fall back into our old nature and be motivated to try harder. Personally, I'm coming to the conclusion that the doctrine of original guilt has perverted our view of God, and removing it may make a huge difference to the way we live!

14

▾

Miracles

Jesus said we can ask for whatever we want and that we only need the smallest grain of faith. So why aren't miracles more common? Some missing words from these phrases provide the key.

One of my favorite pieces of Christian literature is the satirical novel *The Sacred Diary of Adrian Plass Aged 37¾*. I particularly like Adrian's account of his forays into the practicing of miracles. His desire to have faith that will move mountains sees him start out by trying to move a paper clip:

> Had another go with the paper-clip tonight. I really
>   took authority over it. Couldn't get it to budge.
> Told God I'd give up anything he wanted, if he
>   would just make it move half an inch.
> Nothing!
> All rather worrying really. If you only need faith
>   the size of a mustard seed to move a mountain,
>   what hope is there for me when I can't even get
>   a paper-clip to do what it's told?[1]

---

1. Adrian Plass, *The Sacred Diary of Adrian Plass Aged 37¾* (Grand Rapids: Zondervan, 1987), 19.

While the account is fictional, it reflects the experience of many Christians whose heart may be in the right place, but whose theology on this point is somewhat adrift. God is not a vending machine with a slot into which you can put "faith" tokens to purchase miracles. We should learn from Simon "the magician" who was punished for trying to buy the ability to do miracles on demand (Acts 8:9–24).

Yet Jesus *did* say: "Have faith. ... If anyone says to this mountain, 'Go, throw yourself into the sea,' ... it will be done for them. Therefore I tell you, whatever you ask for in prayer, believe that you have received it, and it will be yours" (Mark 11:22–24).

Verses such as these have led people to think that miracles are a matter of commanding things to happen, so the only reason healing or other wonders fail to happen is that we don't get the command right—perhaps we don't have enough faith. Some unscrupulous "faith healers" have become rich by offering to pray in return for a donation and then blaming the donor's "lack of faith" when it doesn't work. But doesn't this verse say it *should* work?

FAITH IN A PERSON

It is helpful to remember that Christian faith is in a person: in God himself. In recent years, the meaning of the word "faith" has changed somewhat. We can now talk about having faith in ourselves as if faith is some kind of assertive willpower, but this is entirely different from its meaning in the Bible. One way to make sure we don't misunderstand "faith" in the Bible is to always mentally expand it to "faith *in God*." So, when it says, "have faith," read it as "have faith in God." Jesus even does that for us in the verse I've quoted above, which actually starts: "Have faith in God ..." (Mark 11:22).

When Jesus encouraged people to have faith in God, it some-times sounds as if he was saying they needed this faith *in order* to be healed. For example: "Your faith has healed you" (Mark 5:34; 10:52). He meant that we need to have "faith *in God*"—that is, we need to trust *him*. The people who were healed in the Gospels sometimes had no faith. When the paralytic was lowered through the roof, Jesus noted that his friends had faith—but this isn't said of the ill person himself (Mark 2:5). On other occasions the person being healed certainly had no faith—such as the Temple guard whose ear Jesus reattached (Luke 22:49–51). And in many healings (nine out of twenty-eight that are recorded) there is no specific mention of faith, except the implied faith of Jesus. When we understand "faith" as meaning "faith *in God*," this all makes sense: Jesus attributed all healings to *God*, not to our faith. So when he castigated his disciples for having "no faith"—such as when their boat was sinking in a storm (Mark 4:40)—he was telling them to have faith *in God*, and not to con-jure up more faith inside themselves.

Like so many of us, the disciples didn't understand this at first, so they asked Jesus to "increase" their faith (Luke 17:5). Perhaps groaning inwardly at their stupidity, Jesus explained that they only needed faith the size of a mustard seed—that is, the tiniest amount imaginable. Today he might say that an atom of faith is all that's needed. There only needs to be enough faith to indicate the direction of our faith—because even the tiniest amount of faith directed toward God shows that our trust is in *him*. The size of our faith doesn't matter because the power lies in how great God is, not how great our faith is.

MOVING MOUNTAINS

What did Jesus mean about throwing mountains into the sea? This teaching followed immediately after he made a fig tree wither because it didn't have any fruit (Mark 11:12–24). The meaning becomes clear in the next two chapters of Mark if we bear in mind that "the mountain of the Lord" is a metaphor for the temple. It is used in this way about two dozen times in the Old Testament (e.g., Isa 2:2–3; 11:9; 40:4, 9; 56:7). Jesus cited one of those verses just before he threw out the money-changers: "my holy mountain ... my house will be called a house of prayer" (Isa 56:7 = Mark 11:17).

Mark 11 and 12 chart the growing opposition to Jesus (11:15–33; 12:13–40), Jesus' prediction that the Jewish leaders would be thrown out of "the vineyard" (12:1–12), and his predictions that the Temple would be destroyed (13:1–27). Jesus then used the fig tree as an illustration of what was to come: "Now learn this lesson from the fig-tree: As soon as its twigs get tender and its leaves come out, you know that summer is near. Even so, when you see these things happening, you know that it is near" (13:28–29). Jesus concluded that its destruction would happen within a generation (13:30–37)—which it did, in AD 70. He had called on God to do the impossible—to throw down his own mountain, his own fruitless fig tree—and it happened. Jesus wasn't telling his disciples to make showy or frivolous demands of God by moving mountains. He was teaching them to pray for the things that God has already said he wants to do to advance his kingdom, even when they seem as impossible as the destruction of the Jerusalem Temple, which had served its purpose.

Another phrase that gets misunderstood is the apparent promise that you will receive "whatever you ask for." In the same way that we have to mentally expand "faith" in the Bible to "faith *in God,*" we have to mentally expand the phrase "whatever you ask for" to "whatever you ask for *in Jesus' name.*" John actually does this for us repeatedly (John 14:13; 14; 15:16; 16:23–26), though not every single time because it becomes rather repetitive. John frequently includes these extra words to explain what it means: when we ask God for something, we are asking as servants of Jesus. This means we don't ask for whatever we feel like having: we ask for things that Jesus wants.

In the ancient world, everyone understood this distinction because they knew how a servant should act—they saw slaves every day. Modern readers can perhaps imagine a personal assistant or a butler ordering a limo for a journey or a perhaps ordering a new car from a showroom. They order it *in the name* of their boss, not for themselves. If they started ordering such things for themselves, they'd soon be fired. Perhaps one reason why John added "in Jesus' name" so often is that the early church needed the same reminder that we do: when we pray we are working in God's service, not self-service.

MIRACLES ON DEMAND

Another thing that doesn't come across in English is that prayer is a request, not a demand. In older English, the word "pray" still carried the connotation of asking or even begging, as in "pray tell," or when Shakespeare's Romeo says to the priest: "This I pray, that thou consent to marry us today." So when we "pray" to God, it makes no sense to express it as a demand or a shopping list, because in that case it isn't a "prayer" any more.

A common word that's often left untranslated in the Old Testament is *na*, which means something like "please." The word *na* occurs so often in polite or reverential Hebrew that it would look silly to add "please" everywhere, so we don't see it in English translations. One place it is found is at the end of the phrase "Hosanna," which we should perhaps translate as "save us *please*." However, translators felt there was no need to include "please" because this is implied by the fact that prayer is always a plea or polite request—it can never be a demand.

So, when Paul prayed about his "thorn in the flesh," he wasn't disconcerted when God didn't remove it (2 Cor 12:7–9). He simply prayed again, a few times. Probably this was a deteriorating eye condition, which would be disastrous for a Bible scholar (see Gal 4:15; 6:11). We'd expect it to be God's will to heal it, but that didn't happen. Similarly, Paul no doubt prayed for his coworker Epaphras to get better, and yet he continued to be ill and almost died, though he recovered eventually (Phil 2:25–30). The point is that although Paul had often prayed and seen God heal instantaneously (Acts 19:11–12), he didn't presume it would *always* happen.

Paul served God, not the other way around. When we pray for healing, we aren't putting our faith in a vending machine or in an online order form; we put our faith in God. Usually we don't know exactly what God's plan is, like Paul didn't when he prayed about his thorn. After praying three times he stopped— not because he lacked faith, but because he realized this healing was not part of God's will for him (2 Cor 12:9).

This acceptance of God's will must have been really hard for Paul. He had perhaps seen blind people healed and knew that God could help him—and yet God left him with this thorn! Some have turned away from God in circumstances like this, and Paul's simple acceptance of his illness in this way impresses me greatly. It's easy to have faith in God when life is comfortable or prayers are always answered in the way we want. It is much harder to trust God when those prayers appear to be unheard. One day we will understand God's reasons, but until then, like Paul, we should put our faith in God, pray in Jesus' name, and patiently accept the outcome, whatever it is.

15

▾

Prayer

What's the point of telling God what he already knows or trying to change his mind? In a glimpse behind the scenes, the Bible shows that prayer helps align spiritual forces with God's will.

Does prayer work? Christians agree that it does—but who or what does it work *on*? Since God sees everything, the purpose of prayer can't be to tell God things that he doesn't know about. So is prayer trying to change God's mind about what he should do? Or trying to change the minds of others, for example by making them decide to follow Jesus? The idea that we can somehow persuade God to change his mind or that God interferes with people's free will is hugely problematic.

One common conclusion is that prayer only changes us. That is, when we pray, it changes *our* minds. When we pray about something, we may, for example, suddenly realize how we could help in a situation or accept the situation as part of God's will, so that prayer helps us to cope with it. This is undoubtedly true on many occasions, but the Bible makes it clear that prayers often also result in dramatic changes to a situation.

The doctrine of prayer as presented in the Bible suggests that God works as a result of prayer, on the world around us and *also* on ourselves. Prayers in the Psalms often request God's strength to cope with a situation. However, these Psalms usually *also* include requests that God should step in and change things. In the Bible, prayer is a way of getting things done by divine intervention—affecting both the person praying *and* the situation they are praying about.

I'd better admit it: I often do pray as though I want God to reconsider what he appears to be doing—as if I know better than he does. But didn't Moses do this? He asked for God's mercy on the Israelites after they'd built the golden calf (Exod 32:11-13), and Psalm 106:23 says that Moses "stood in the breach"—that is, his prayer plugged the gap in the defenses for the nation. But did that prayer change God's mind? In Ezekiel 22:30 God said that he longed for someone to stand in the breach again for Israel, "but I found no one." In that situation at least, the prayers were working to further God's will, not to change it, because Ezekiel said that God was longing for someone to stand in the breach like Moses did—that is, he wanted someone to bring about that change in God's action by praying!

PRAYER AS WORK

The Bible gives only a few small hints about how prayer works. It suggests that our prayers actually change things directly—with God's permission or help, of course. That is, our prayers are part of the work that is needed in order to accomplish God's will. Prayers aren't needed to persuade God that he should do something; they are somehow being used by God to get that thing done. We'll turn to the biblical evidence shortly, but first it is interesting to realize how many problems are solved when we understand prayer in this way.

It explains the apparent contradiction in Jesus' teaching on prayer when on one hand he tells us to keep on praying, but on the other he urges us not to pray with empty repetitions. For example, he says we shouldn't just keep on talking at God, "for your Father knows what you need before you ask him" (Matt 6:8), and yet he says we should "always pray and not give up" like a persistent widow nagging a lazy judge (Luke 18:1–5). So God knows what we need, but he still wants us to pray persistently for things that are *already* his will. This persistence makes sense if our ongoing prayers are actually helping to bring God's will into effect. This also fits in with the emphasis on praying "your will be done" (e.g., Matt 6:10; 26:39) and praying "in my name." Somehow, we are getting God's will done by praying for it.

So how does God answer prayer? It's an old joke that you'll have heard many times before, but I'm going to tell it again: A man prays, "O Lord, you know the mess I'm in, please let me win the lottery." The next week, he prays again, and this time he's complaining, "O Lord, didn't you hear my prayer last week? I'll lose everything I hold dear unless I win the lottery." The third week, he prays again and this time he's desperate, "O Lord, this is the third time I've prayed to you to let me win the lottery! I ask and I plead and still you don't help me!" Suddenly a booming voice sounds from heaven: "My son, my son, be reasonable. Meet me halfway. Buy a lottery ticket!"

That joke illustrates an important aspect of how prayer works. We might imagine that God does everything by direct action—by snapping his fingers like a genie or thinking things into existence. But the Bible also describes lots of things being done *for* God, by people or by angels. So if we have a part to play in answering a prayer, we should get on and do it!

PRAYER AS A FIGHT

Daniel gives us an intriguing insight into what actually happens when we pray. He decided to pray seriously about the future of Israel, which was in exile in Babylon. His fasting and prayers continued for three weeks before an angel arrived with an answer. The angel also gave Daniel an explanation for the delay: "Since the first day ... your words were heard, and I have come in response to them. But the prince of the Persian kingdom resisted me twenty-one days. Then Michael, one of the chief princes, came to help me, because I was detained there with the king of Persia" (Dan 10:12-13). These "princes" appear to be angels because one of them is Michael, the angel over Israel (see 12:1). So the answer to Daniel's prayer was delayed by the interference of an enemy angel!

It seems that prayer can be a battle against spiritual evil. There is no way of telling how metaphorical this account is, but we can see that Daniel's prayer was meeting resistance. The implication is that if he hadn't persisted, the answer would not have come. So Daniel became an essential part of that battle by continuing to pray. In that kind of situation, Jesus' teaching on persistence in prayer makes sense because it is actively affecting the situation—even when we can't yet see it.

Even praying for people to be saved is portrayed as engagement in a battle. Paul said that when unconverted people read the Bible, they can't see the truth because there's a "veil" over their eyes, but the Holy Spirit gives them freedom to understand (2 Cor 3:14-17). That freedom is what we pray for, so that they can decide to follow Jesus. We aren't praying to change their minds—because you can't *make* someone fall in love, even with Jesus—and we aren't trying to change God's mind because he already wants all to be saved. Our prayers are battling the evil one who wants to keep them blinded by that veil.

Not all prayer concerns combating evil. Even if God answers it by sending an angel, this doesn't mean that it involves a spiritual struggle. When the church prayed for Peter in prison, an angel was sent to release him, but this is not described as a battle of any kind. Those who were praying didn't know that would happen—they were as surprised as he was (see Acts 12:6–16). They simply prayed to God and left him to work out how to use those prayers. How prayer works behind the scenes is no doubt a complex matter, and it won't always work in the same way. For instance, it may sometimes cause an angel to do something, or it may prevent some spiritual evil. Our prayers may power a slow progress or trigger a quick release, so some prayers take very little time to be answered, and others take longer for a variety of reasons.

However, a "delay" in prayer being answered is not always due to something invisible happening in the background, as in the cases of Daniel and Peter. We should be aware that some-times the delay means we are praying for the wrong thing, as Paul realized with regard to his thorn (2 Cor 12:7–9). But we don't have to worry about these complexities because prayer is a simple request directed to God, and he figures out how to use it. We shouldn't be tempted to try bending the forces of nature or communicating with angels (Col 2:18). Even Daniel, who was very aware of angels, still directed his prayer to God himself (Dan 10:12).

PRAYER CHANGES THINGS

Prayer isn't just for recluses. Paul was a pragmatic and fero-ciously active believer who wasn't put off by shipwrecks, life-threatening punishments, or opposition. But he prayed as seriously as any contemplative hermit or passive visionary and urged others to pray for him: "Pray in the Spirit on all occasions with all kinds of prayers and requests ... be alert and always keep on praying" (Eph 6:18).

Because we pray directly to God, prayer really does change *things*. It isn't just about aligning our minds with the will of God; it aligns *the world* with the will of God. God isn't inviting us to give him a wish list; he is inviting us to be his agents in bringing about his will. When we pray "Your will be done on earth," we aren't muttering a pious hope: we are actually helping to achieve it.

All this means we might achieve much more for God if we change the busy schedules that stop us from praying. As John Wesley said, "Prayer is where the action is."

16

▾

Omnipotence

How does God achieve his plans? Does he manipulate us like a puppet master, corner us like a chess player, or guide and protect us from evil like a warrior?

How many times have you heard "If God is all-powerful and good, then why is there so much suffering?" The question is older than Job, who ponders this in the Bible. Like most of us, Job makes the mistake of concentrating on the nature of suffering rather than the power of God. The answer lies in God's sovereignty and omnipotence, because the question is: how does God carry out his purpose?

After God created a perfect universe, sin entered and spoiled it, but God has said that he will reign with justice and fill the earth with peace and the full glory of his presence (Isa 11:1–9). Whatever God wants to happen *will* happen, because the Bible declares that he is all-powerful (1 Chr 29:11–12; Job 42:2; Matt 19:26; Eph 1:19–21).[1] All Christians believe that nothing can prevent God from carrying from out his plan—but what is his method for attaining this goal?

---

1. The Greek word meaning "all-powerful" (*pantodunamos*) does not actually occur in the Bible, though there are ten occurrences of "all-authority" (*pantokratos*—e.g., Rev 4:8), which is usually translated "almighty."

Some theologians regard God like a puppet master who moves every person and every atom exactly as he wishes. Others liken him to a chess player who manipulates some pieces in order to encourage or constrain other pieces to move into the positions he has planned for them. Still others think that God is like a great warrior who fights negative forces to enable people to move in the direction he wants. All three strategies will result in God achieving his plan, and of course he can use any strategy that he wishes. But which is the most biblically accurate image of how he exercises his control?

GOD AT THE EXODUS

The Bible includes texts that seem to support all three, but for a correct understanding it is important that we consider these in context. The best way to understand which one applies is to look for texts that could be interpreted in any of these three ways and then see which interpretation best fits the context. For example, we could interpret the story of the exodus as God working like a puppet master because he hardened Pharaoh's heart and then punished him for it. On the other hand, we could also interpret the events as God working like a chess player, controlling coincidences so that Moses' basket floated past Pharaoh's daughter just when she was bathing. Or we could say that God acted like a warrior, conquering the Egyptians. This is how Miriam and Moses praised him: "The Lord is a warrior; the Lord is his name. Pharaoh's chariots and his army he has hurled into the sea" (Exod 15:3–4). I don't think Moses would regard the other two images as wrong, because it seems that God has no single method. He strategizes like a chess player, he controls like a puppet master, and he fights for us.

Actually, Pharaoh is not a very good example of a puppet because sometimes he hardened his own heart and sometimes

God hardened it (e.g., Exod 9:34; 10:1). These two descriptions suggest that Pharaoh hardened his own resolve and God helped him stick with his decision. In this case, Pharaoh isn't like puppet because a puppet has no resolve. Instead, God is portrayed like a chess player who encourages his opponent to carry out an ill-conceived strategy! This doesn't mean that the view of a totally controlling God is wrong, but it isn't what the text portrays at this point.

The image of God as a warrior is very common in the Old Testament. He fights for his people against spiritual enemies and helps them fight physical enemies. We see this in Israel's political history, in the prophetic visions, and even in poetic praise. The psalmist says that God is a fortress and defense when we are attacked, a rescuer and redeemer when we are captured, and the victor at the end of every battle (e.g., Pss 46; 59; 62).

If God fights for and rescues his people, this implies that previously they have been suffering. This suffering included violent attacks, defeat, capture, illnesses, betrayal by friends, famines, and sudden poverty. The psalmists and prophets constantly praise God for delivering his people from such suffering. In other words, the Bible does not portray God as preventing suffering, but instead it portrays God helping his people when disasters have occurred. Sometimes he rescues them from that disaster, while at other times he helps them cope with the suffering till it ends.

THE COMPLEXITY OF GOD'S STRATEGY

These three different viewpoints of how God acts imply different reasons why he allows his people to suffer. If he is a puppet master, we have to conclude that every disaster is intentional and that he wishes to impose injury, illness, and disease on his people for some reason. This might be for a variety of reasons:

perhaps he wants them to be grateful when he "rescues" them, or perhaps he wants them to depend on him, so he only rescues them when they pray.

If, however, he is a chess player, he could use disasters to move people into situations he wants them to be in for a variety of reasons. We might conclude that he isn't very expert at this, because he lets himself lose so many pieces—people can be harmed in the process! However, any chess player knows that the game progresses by losing pieces. In the New Testament, Paul recognized that God does sometimes acts like a chess player—such as when God closed some doors and opened others in order to direct him to Macedonia (Acts 16:6–10). And sometimes Paul regarded God like a puppet master—for example, God's hardening of Pharaoh's heart (in Rom 9:17–18); though we must remember that Paul knew (just as we do) that Pharaoh also hardened his own heart.

But most often, Paul regarded God as a warrior and victor—as someone who redeems and rescues his people from principalities and powers (see Rom 8:37–39). In fact, Paul boasted about the suffering he went through: shipwrecks, beatings, and even stoning (2 Cor 11:23–30). In his Prison Epistles, he didn't wonder why he was suffering; instead he rejoiced in being able to suffer for Jesus! He regarded suffering as negligible in the light of the final victory (2 Cor 4:17). God's sovereignty in the Bible is magnified when, like Paul, his people continue to follow and trust him even though they are going through hardship.

God's strategy is complex and mostly hidden—we certainly cannot see it in full yet—but the Bible gives us some valuable glimpses into what he is doing, and we can see his hand everywhere. From illnesses to armed opponents, we can rely on God to give us strength to help us cope or to rescue us in the timing of his planning. Meanwhile we wait: we wait for the final victory and for the end of all suffering. Then we will be able to peep behind the curtain and see how he actually did achieve his plans.

17

▼

Providence

Romans didn't believe that bad things happened by chance—they believed in a goddess called Fortuna or "Luck." But what does the Bible say about random chance and divine purpose? And how does God work all things for good for his followers?

Florence Nightingale's superiors were aghast when she ordered medical supplies for the Crimean War in advance by predicting the number of men who would become injured or diseased. They held the belief that because humans act with free will and, on top of that, God does what he wants, it was simply not possible for the future to be predicted. How could anyone forecast the percentage of men who would be injured in a cavalry charge, or the proportion who would get malaria? Nevertheless, Nightingale's predictions were proved correct and, because of them, fewer men died. The importance of the study of medical statistics was recognized from that point on.

Throughout history people have believed that things did not depend on mere chance. Ancient Greeks believed in the Fates, who had control of each person's destiny, spinning the threads of their life and deciding its length. Ancient Romans worshiped the goddess Fortuna, though she wasn't always helpful—she spun a wheel at random to determine good or bad circumstances for you. This "Lady Luck" remained popular even among Christians, who transformed the blessing "Good luck" into "Godspeed" ("spede" was Middle English for "luck"). From the time of Augustine in the fifth century, the church tried to suppress such phrases as superstition, but failed. In John Wesley's journal for 1763, he records a group of ministers wishing him "Good luck in the name of the Lord," and few Christians today would regard saying "Good luck" as pagan.

The Old Testament writers believed that God was in charge of everything. Even throwing a lot (which was like flipping a coin) did not give a random result because they believed God was in overall control (Prov 16:33). However, they also recognized the opposite—that things did appear to happen by chance at times. When an arrow killed King Ahab, it looked like random bad luck. He was disguised as a normal soldier, so no one aimed at him in particular, and the arrow just happened to hit a vulnerable slit in his armor at the right angle to penetrate it. The original text says of the archer who killed him, "he drew his bow innocently"—which is as near as Hebrew can express the idea of an unplanned, random event (1 Kgs 22:34). Yet the reason Ahab was disguised was that a prophet had predicted that he would be killed in the battle—so this apparently random event was actually controlled by God.

Does this mean that God decides where every raindrop falls and where every germ infects?

HUMAN FREEDOM

Some Christian thinkers regard the world as completely mechanistic—that is, God set everything going and now simply lets things happen according to the laws of science. Others believe God may intervene with a miracle very occasionally. At the other end of this spectrum are Christian thinkers who say that God directs and decides every single event, down to the atomic level.

But if God directs absolutely everything, it is difficult to find room for human freedom. It would seem pointless to pray, because God has already decided what he will do and even what he will make us want to pray for. And God would have determined exactly what we are thinking right now. (It all gets very confusing!) For such reasons, most Christian thinkers hold a view somewhere in the middle of these extremes. They believe that God works in the world alongside the laws of nature, while allowing human freedom; that he occasionally interrupts normality by doing something we regard as a miracle; and that he often works in the background in ways we usually don't notice.

Jesus appears to have had this middle view. This is, of course, a strange way to talk about Jesus, partly because this spectrum of thinking about providence wasn't clear until much later and partly because we can't pigeonhole Jesus! Nevertheless, in the Gospels Jesus assumes that God was involved in every detail, while at the same time he implies that effective prayer and human freedom are realities. He encourages his followers to pray not only for big things such as healing but also little things such as daily food, because he assumes that God can influence everything.

On the other hand, Jesus told his followers to pray that the predicted assault on Jerusalem wouldn't be on a Sabbath, when it would be more difficult to flee (Matt 24:20). This implies that either the exact day wasn't yet decided or Jesus didn't know it. Of course, it is quite possible that he didn't know this detail, because he was a real human with a finite brain, though presumably God could tell him any specific detail he needed to know. However, Jesus wouldn't urge his followers to pray about something that was already decided, because that would be pointless. Or, if prayer *was* required to help bring it about, he would have told them which day to pray for it to happen on. This little command by Jesus gives us a valuable insight into how God works. He will achieve all his purposes, but he works alongside his people, and he reacts to what his enemies do, until his will is achieved.

Jesus thought differently from most Jews of his day about this. They believed that everything was specifically purposed by God, but Jesus denied this—at least, he denied that we could *know* the purpose of most events. For example, when he was asked about the people who were killed when a tower collapsed in Siloam, Jesus' answer was the opposite of what most would have thought: he said that those who were killed were no worse sinners than others (Luke 13:4–5). On another occasion, when he was asked whether a man was blind because of his own sin or his parents' sin, Jesus said that it was due to neither, though his illness would bring glory to God; then, to prove it, Jesus healed him (John 9:2–7). In other words, the bad things that had happened were not part of God's plan of reward or retribution, but we could still learn from them.

Old Testament prophets said that God picks and chooses which towns to send rain on (Amos 4:7; Jer 14:22). However, this doesn't mean that he *always* does this. The story of Elijah suggests that sometimes God creates a drought to show his displeasure or ends a drought to help those who trust him (1 Kgs 17:1; 18:1). Normally, though, rain falls indiscriminately, as Jesus said: God sends rain (and drought) equally on the just and unjust (Matt 5:45).

However, the first Christians taught that even when things go wrong, God is with us and can turn it to good: "In all things God works for the good of those who love him" (Rom 8:28). That is, God can bring some good out of whatever happens—even out of the bad things. Some older Bibles unfortunately mask this message by translating "God works all things for good," which could be interpreted as "God makes sure that only good things happen." This interpretation is quickly proved wrong by real life—except, perhaps, for those who are very rich, very healthy, and very "lucky"! Another, and equally wrong, way this has been interpreted is to suggest that the bad things that happen to us are sent by God for some higher purpose that we won't understand this side of eternity.

BAD THINGS HAPPEN TO EVERYBODY

Why do bad things happen? Is everyone, including Christians, subject to "bad luck" (i.e., random disasters)? The Bible doesn't ultimately answer this, but we do learn that God is with us in all things. Paul pointed out that we live in a fallen world marred by sin, which is groaning in pain until Jesus comes, so we shouldn't be surprised that things go wrong (Rom 8:19-25).

Ever since Adam introduced disobedience and other evils, our lives have been different from what God intended. He wanted us to live forever in Eden. God didn't want *any* bad things to happen to us, but Adam sinned, and so do we. However, despite our disobedience, the world isn't out of God's control. He can help us get through bad times, and he can turn bad experiences into an important lesson or use it in a way to strengthen us. Sometimes he may miraculously rescue us. God is still in charge, because even though the world is fallen, he is still able to bring good out of evil. The cross is the ultimate example of this—the ultimate evil being turned by God into the ultimate good.

The cross was not a matter of chance. God decided to rescue a planet-full of people, and he did so. Whether chance or human freedom exist, God will do what he plans to do. So perhaps wishing someone "good luck" is completely pagan, because this blessing is addressed to Lady Luck, not to God. It is much better to say "Praying for you!"—especially if it is true!

18

▾

Unforgivable Sin

Jews believed that the sin of blasphemy was unforgivable, and although Jesus took this belief seriously, he also offered a solution. But what does Hebrews mean when it refers to a sinner who cannot be brought to repent?

I'm sure I'm not the only church leader to experience a very particular kind of sinking feeling when someone approaches and says: "I think I've committed the unforgivable sin." Their terrible burden of guilt may come from something they've done, perhaps long in the past. Often, no amount of reassurance of God's forgiveness will remove it.

For the Jews listening to Jesus' words recorded in Matthew 12:31-32; Mark 3:28-29; and Luke 12:8-10, his mention of an unforgiveable sin wouldn't have prompted any surprise, because they knew all about this. They already believed that the sin of using God's name in a derogatory way was unforgivable. They concluded this from the unique and terrible warning in the Ten Commandments: "The Lord will not hold anyone guiltless who misuses his name" (Exod 20:7 = Deut 5:11). These words didn't occur with regard to any other command, so presumably the others *could* be forgiven if you repented.

REVILING GOD

This "misuse" of God's name wasn't simply speaking the name—you had to use it in a derisory or reviling way—that is, in what we now call a "blasphemous" way. The text is a little confusing to us because the Greek verb *blasphemeō* means "to revile/slander," so it can refer to humans as well as God. For example, it is used when Paul was "reviled" (Acts 13:45; 18:6). This explains the strange phrase "all manner of sin and blasphemy shall be forgiven" (Matt 12:31 KJV), which is much more helpfully translated in the NIV: "every kind of sin and slander can be forgiven."

When Jesus told his hearers that reviling the Holy Spirit was unforgivable, the Jews listening to him realized he was referring to the sin of reviling God, because they knew that this was the only sin that was unforgivable. Jesus said (paraphrasing Mark 3:28-29): "You can revile anyone and it will be forgiven, but you'll not be forgiven if you revile ..." Now, at this point, his Jewish audience would have expected him to say "God," but he said something shocking instead: "You'll not be forgiven if you revile *the Holy Spirit*." By saying this, Jesus was declaring that the Holy Spirit is God. Only God is so great that reviling him could not be forgiven, so if the same is true about the Holy Spirit, then he, too, must be God. This concept was something completely new and difficult for the Jews. They knew about the Holy Spirit (he is mentioned in Ps 51 and Isaiah, as well as in rabbinic writings), but they regarded him as separate from God.

FORGIVING THE UNFORGIVABLE

Some Jewish rabbis were puzzled that the Ten Commandments could include a sin that God didn't forgive even when someone repented. The problem was "solved" by Rabbi Ishmael ben Elisha in the second century by concluding it was forgiven at their death. All other repented sins were forgiven at the Day of

Atonement, but you remained guilty of this terrible sin throughout your life until the day you died. This solution meant that it
was still true that "the Lord will not hold anyone guiltless" for
this sin, though a repentant person could be forgiven at their
death. However, Christians didn't need to resort to this kind of
reasoning, because they knew there was a better solution to all
sin.

Christians don't rely on the Day of Atonement or other sacrifices to deal with their sins. For Christians, all repented sins
are now covered by Jesus' sacrifice, so they are all forgivable—
even the sin of blasphemy. So for Christians, there is no unforgivable sin.

One curiosity in this passage is that Jesus didn't include himself and even denied that those who reviled "the Son of Man"
were committing this unforgivable sin (Matt 12:32). My guess is
that he didn't expect anyone to recognize his divinity until after
his resurrection, so at that point he didn't class this as the same
kind of sin. After Jesus had conquered death, such doubt was no
longer an excuse. Jesus' divinity became plain even to Thomas,
who declared: "My Lord and my God" (John 20:28).

REFUSING TO REPENT

There is another passage in Hebrews that could possibly be
interpreted to refer to an unforgivable sin, because it says
that some people can't be persuaded to repent of their sin: "It
is impossible for those who ... have fallen away, to be brought
back to repentance" (Heb 6:4, 6). Later the author points out
how serious it is to reject Jesus now that he has died and risen:
"No sacrifice for sins is left" for those who "deliberately keep on
sinning" because, in effect, they have "trampled the Son of God
underfoot" (Heb 10:26, 29). The individuals described in this
passage knew about Jesus, and knew that he died for their sins,

yet they still choose to deliberately keep committing those sins while relying on Jesus' willingness to forgive them. This is like someone who keeps stealing, knowing that his brother will willingly take the blame each time and bear the punishment for it. The writer to the Hebrews says that such people are "crucifying the Son of God all over again" (6:6).

Such people, as Hebrews says, can't "be brought back to repentance." You can't explain the truth to them because they already know it, and you can't persuade them because they have firmly decided to reject it. Of course, this doesn't mean that they can't "come back" by themselves, but it does mean that there is no way that we will be able to persuade them. However, we can still pray for them, because the Holy Spirit can work in their hearts in a way that we can't, though God is not going to force them to love him against their will.

These passages are particularly difficult for individuals who have irrational feelings of guilt, because, to explain this feeling, they believe they must have committed some kind of sin that cannot be forgiven. But they are completely different from the people described in Hebrews. These people have rejected God consciously and intentionally—the verb "fall away" that is used in Hebrews 6:6 stands out as the first active verb after a series of passive ones to emphasize that this was their deliberate decision.

If someone *wants* to repent to God, then this is proof that they aren't one of those being described in Hebrews. Unfortunately, for some people, even when this is pointed out to them, their overwhelming feeling of guilt continues. However often they repent of their sin to Jesus, their Lord and Savior, it is impossible to convince them that their sin is forgiven. This shows that the feeling of guilt isn't due to conviction by the Holy Spirit, because in that case it would disappear when they repent. The promise to us all is that "if we confess our sins, he is faithful and just and will forgive us our sins and purify us from all unrighteousness" (1 John 1:9). So the Holy Spirit will not continue to prompt us with feelings of guilt after we have confessed our sin. Therefore, if we continue to feel guilt, this is likely to be due to depression or some other cause of general low self-esteem—it is not from the Holy Spirit.

Repentance is the infallible path to forgiveness. If you want to repent of your sin to God, then you can be sure that you have not committed the terrible sin referred to in Hebrews, because the person who *has* committed this sin does not want to repent. And when we repent, we can be sure that God's arms, like the arms of the prodigal's father, are always open to welcome us, even if we are repenting of something we have tried to stop many times before. God is *always* willing to forgive the repentant sinner who wants to follow him.

19

▾

Hell

Jesus taught a great deal about hell as a place where people were tormented, though the Epistles speak mainly about destruction in hell. When Jesus referred to eternal punishment, did this mean torment or destruction—or both?

I t's not fair" is an all-too familiar phrase that children use before they learn that life simply *isn't* fair. What begins as a cry for justice turns into a resigned silence—or sometimes even a quest for personal revenge. Parents try to explain to them that God will bring real justice, but then they may learn the traditional church teaching on hell and discover that all sin—however big or small—results in the same punishment. According to this teaching, a shoplifter who doesn't repent will be punished in exactly the same way as a multiple-rapist or murderer who doesn't repent. Like Abraham, we'd love to say to God: "Far be it from you! Will not the Judge of all the earth do right?" (Gen 18:25). We want to shout out to him, "It's not fair!"

Many people today are horrified by this teaching because eternal punishment in hell seems disproportionate for all but a few utterly evil people. It is a subject that we do not often hear preached on today—perhaps because it is so offensive. But does it reflect what the New Testament teaches?

THE NATURE OF HELL

Hell was an important part of Jesus' teaching, and we hear more about hell from him than any other Jew of his time. Jesus had to speak about hell so much because he disagreed fundamentally with Jewish teaching on it. He told his hearers that unless they personally repented, they were all going to hell (Luke 13:28). This was completely opposite from what most Jews believed.

Normal Jewish teaching about hell in the time of Jesus is illustrated in a parable told by a rabbi called Johanan ben Zakkai. He is significant because his forty-year ministry in Galilee overlapped with the time when Jesus was preaching and teaching there, so Jesus probably heard Johanan himself tell this parable:

> A king invited all his people to a banquet but did not say when it would start. The wise people put on their fine clothes and waited at the door of the palace saying "Surely a royal palace already has everything ready." The foolish people carried on with their work saying, "Surely a banquet takes time to prepare." Suddenly the king called in the people; the wise entered in fine clothes but the foolish entered in dirty clothes. The king rejoiced at the wise but was angry with the fools. He ordered: "Let those who dressed for the banquet sit and feast, but those who did not dress for the banquet will stand and watch them."[1]

This parable reflected the common Jewish belief that all Jews would go to heaven, but they would not all receive equal honor—the fools didn't share the honor (i.e., the food) that the wise enjoyed.

---

1. Babylonian Talmud Shabbat 153a (TinyURL.com/ZakkaiBanquet).

The Gospels record forty-five verses on hell, which is a lot considering that there are only sixty-five verses on love. Some of Jesus' teaching on hell was appended to parables very similar to the one told by Johanan. He talked about people being invited to a king's banquet, wise and foolish girls waiting with lamps outside a wedding, and a man being thrown out of a banquet for not being properly dressed (Matt 22:2–10 = Luke 14:16–24; Matt 25:1–13; 22:11–14). In each of these, he contradicted Johanan's well-known parable in one important way: many people are *excluded* from the banquet—they aren't ready and arrive after the doors are closed; they decide themselves not to go; or they are thrown out. In Johanan's version, everyone (i.e., every Jew) is admitted into heaven.

Jesus was also very clear about the fate of those left "outside" the banquet. He depicts hell as eternal fire, weeping, and teeth-clenching pain (Matt 5:22; 7:19; 8:12, 41, 50; 13:42, 50; 18:8; 22:13; 24:51; 25:30, 41; Mark 9:43, 48; Luke 13:28; John 15:6). These images were not invented by Jesus; they were already used by other Jews, who likened hell to a place called Gehenna, where there was eternal fire and worms. No one hearing Jesus teach would have thought that this was a literal description of hell because Gehenna was the name of a valley just outside Jerusalem that they'd seen for themselves. No homes were built in this southwestern corner of the city because it was where babies had been burned to death as sacrifices on the altars of Molech (2 Kgs 23:10). Later Jewish sources say that smoke rose out of cracks in the ground (which presumably made people think it was the entrance to hell) and that rubbish was dumped there.

The fire, smoke, and worms (i.e., maggots) were therefore literal, but they weren't a literal depiction of hell. If hell is literally full of fire and maggots, then heaven is literally full of "harpers harping with their harps" (in the wonderful language of the King

James of Rev 14:2). Thankfully, these are only pictures or metaphors of something we can't describe. Jesus presumably used the same imagery for hell as other Jews because he agreed with the ideas it expressed—that hell is an appalling place.

THE DURATION OF HELL

Is the punishment of hell eternal? Most Jews in Jesus' day thought some people would spend a very short time in hell and then go to heaven. An early tradition says:

> There are three groups:
>
> one group for eternal life—these are the perfectly righteous;
>
> one group for shame and eternal contempt—these are the perfectly evil;
>
> an in-between group—these go down to Gehenna, squeal, then rise from there and are healed.[2]

We can be sure that this was believed by the vast majority of Jews because even the Hillelites and Shammaites, who normally disagreed with each other at every possible opportunity, both accepted this was true. However, the sect at Qumran who wrote the Dead Sea Scrolls disagreed. They said that everyone who goes down to hell is punished for eternity:

> The judgment of all who walk in such ways will be multiple afflictions at the hand of all the angels of perdition,

---

2. My translation of Tosefta Sanhedrin 13:3 (TinyURL.com/ToseftaHell).

everlasting damnation in the wrath of God's furious ven-
geance, never-ending terror and reproach for all eternity,
with a shameful extinction in the fire of Hell's outer darkness. For all their eras, generation by generation, they
will know doleful sorrow, bitter evil and dark happen-
stance, until their utter destruction with neither rem-
nant nor rescue.[3]

It is easy to see what they wanted to emphasize: that the punishment of hell is eternal, so you don't get out of it after a short
period. However, the specific description sounds confusing to
us because they talk about both torment and "extinction in the
fire ... until their utter destruction." They believed in a period
of terrible suffering in hell followed by complete and eternal
destruction.

Jesus clearly agreed with them that those who go to hell stay
there. He emphasized that there are only two ways, to heaven
or hell, and not the third way of possibly leaving hell that other
Jews believed in. People were for him or against him, wheat or
tares, sheep or goats, inside the feasting hall or outside. There
was no middle group of people who stood around the table
watching, or who flit down to hell and back. But did Jesus also
agree with the Qumran sect, which said that people suffer torment in hell and are then destroyed?

Jesus' teaching on eternal punishment is key to the whole
issue. Most New Testament references to eternity with regard
to hell refer to the length of time that hell and its flames will last
(Matt 3:12 = Luke 3:17; Matt 18:8 = Mark 9:43–48; Jude 7), or the
length of time that the devil and his angels will be punished (Rev
12:9; 20:10). There are also a few places where eternity refers

---

3. Rule of the Community column 4, lines 12–14 (TinyURL.com/CommRule).

to the length of time that those who are destroyed will remain destroyed. Isaiah originated the language of worms and fire: "the dead bodies of those who rebelled against me; the worms that eat them will not die, the fire that burns them will not be quenched" (Isa 66:24). And Paul said the unsaved "will be punished with everlasting destruction and shut out from the presence of the Lord" (2 Thess 1:9); and "whoever sows to please their flesh, from the flesh will reap destruction; whoever sows to please the Spirit, from the Spirit will reap eternal life" (Gal 6:8; see also Rom 9:22).

The only verse that unequivocally says that punishment lasts forever is when Jesus gives the moral to his parable of the sheep and the goats: "They will go away to eternal punishment, but the righteous to eternal life" (Matt 25:46). This implies that punishment and reward are equal and opposite: one group experiences eternal life and the other experiences eternal punishment. The type of punishment isn't specified, and the word that is used (*kolasis*) doesn't help us to decide which it is. This word is used elsewhere in Jewish literature to refer to physical suffering and also to "destruction."[4] In one place it is even used for both: Wisdom 19:4 describes the "punishment" of the Egyptian army at the exodus, saying that they suffered both the torments of the plagues and destruction at the Red Sea, which "completed" their punishment. Therefore, the wording of this verse doesn't tell us

---

4. For the meaning "physical suffering," see, e.g., 4 Macc 8:9 NRSV: "But if by disobedience you rouse my anger, you will compel me to destroy each and every one of you with dreadful *punishments* through tortures." For the meaning "destruction," see, e.g., 2 Macc 4:38 NRSV: "Inflamed with anger, he immediately stripped off the purple robe from Andronicus, tore off his clothes, and led him around the whole city to that very place where he had committed the outrage against Onias, and there he dispatched the bloodthirsty fellow. The Lord thus repaid him with the *punishment* he deserved."

whether Jesus understood "eternal punishment" to mean eternal torment, or eternal destruction, or perhaps both.[5]

Personally I think the solution is that Jesus meant both: the "punishment" was suffering followed by destruction. Elsewhere, Jesus clearly speaks about the terrible torment of hell (Matt 8:12; 13:42, 50; 22:13; 24:51; 25:30; Luke 13:28). But he also refers to "destruction" (*apollumi*). This word is sometimes translated "perishing" (e.g., John 3:16, "whoever believes in him shall not perish but have eternal life"; see also Matt 10:28; 18:14), though even in these places it clearly refers to destruction and not to physical death. The same word is used to describe the way that fire destroys chaff, tares, and trees (Matt 3:10, 12; 7:19; 13:30, 40; Luke 3:9, 17), and the death of rebellious servants (Matt 22:7; Mark 12:9).

We saw above that Paul refers to destruction in hell, and so do James and Jude (Jas 4:12; Jude 7). They could learn this from Isaiah, which ends with a vision of the valley outside Jerusalem filled with the dead corpses of those who rebelled, along with everlasting flames and worms (Isa 66:24). If Jesus taught that punishment in hell consists of a period of suffering followed by destruction, then he is in agreement with Paul, James, and Jude.

SUFFERING PROPORTIONAL TO GUILT

To return to the question at the beginning of the chapter: Is eternal torment fair? Unlike some gruesome rabbis and preachers, Jesus didn't describe people suffering in hell for millennia, being prodded by toasting forks in boiling feces—images that are found in Jewish as well as Christian works. Instead, he told a

---

5. Wisdom 19:4 NRSV: "For the fate they deserved drew them on to this end, and made them forget what had happened, in order that they might fill up the *punishment* that their torments still lacked."

parable that implies that suffering will be proportional to guilt. He described a master who returned unexpectedly and found his servants drunk and misbehaving. When the master punished them by beating them, he took into account the amount of each person's guilt: "The servant who knows the master's will and does not get ready or does not do what the master wants will be beaten with many blows. But the one who does not know and does things deserving punishment will be beaten with few blows" (Luke 12:47–48).

This amazing parable tells us not only that suffering in hell will be proportional to the amount of evil committed, but also that it will be proportional to how much a person understood about right and wrong. If they definitely knew their actions were wrong, they will suffer more than if they merely acted thoughtlessly and without deliberation. It is a pity that this is the only mention of proportional punishment that has survived from the teaching of Jesus. However, this isn't surprising, because he wasn't disagreeing with the accepted teaching among Jews. They already believed that God was just and would punish wickedness proportionately, exactly as Abraham had assumed.

However, on the topics where Jesus disagreed with the Jews he had to make his point most emphatically. The Jews thought they were all going to heaven, even if they had to "squeal" in hell for a tiny bit first. Jesus had to make clear to them that there wasn't a "third group" who went to hell first and then heaven— there were only two ways. He also had to emphasize that being a Jew did not guarantee them a place in heaven—they had to personally repent to God.

Jesus' teaching about hell is both frightening and fair. Punishment in hell is final—there is no release into heaven after a period of torment; the period of suffering is followed by eternal destruction. However, the amount of torment is proportional to the amount of sin and guilt. His parable makes clear that the amount of guilt is also determined by how much the person knew. This is presumably why the devil and his angels are tormented forever—because they know exactly what they are doing. So we can agree with Abraham: surely the Judge of all the earth *will* act justly!

Section 3

▼

Doctrines That Matter

20

▾

Trinity

This all-important doctrine can be diminished by simplistic formulae or metaphors, but God is at least as complex as his creation—and certainly more complex than a clover leaf!

W hen Erasmus produced the first printed Greek New Testament in 1516, he left out a part of 1 John now called the "Johannine Comma"—a key prooftext for the Trinity. Here is 1 John 5:7-8, with the part left out in italics: "For there are three that testify *in heaven: the Father, the Word, and the Holy Spirit, and these three are one. And there are three that testify on earth*: the Spirit, the water and the blood; and the three are in agreement."

In his defense, he said this part wasn't in any Greek manuscript, though it had appeared in all the Latin manuscripts since the ninth century. Exasperated by constant criticisms, Erasmus vowed that he would add the verse if anyone could show him even one Greek manuscript that contained it. So someone commissioned monks in Dublin to write one! Erasmus had to keep his vow, as he complained in the notes of his third edition.

Such stories make me feel nervous. Like most biblical scholars, I regard this additional wording as merely a thought that someone noted in the margin of an early Latin manuscript. And, because accidental omissions by scribes were normally added in the margin, those who later copied this particular manuscript mistakenly inserted this marginal note into the text. It's a really wonderful addition, but we don't want to dilute God's word with human thoughts, however useful they are. But for some in Erasmus's day, defending doctrine was more important than their commitment to the exact Bible text. However, does the doctrine of the Trinity really depend on these additional words?

CORE BELIEF

The Trinity is a defining doctrine of Christianity, because those who do not hold to this belief (such as Jehovah's Witnesses and Unitarians) are usually regarded as being outside the universal church. The Nicene Creed—which is accepted by Catholics, Orthodox, and Protestants alike—was crafted especially to define the Trinity. The majority of it deals with the three persons of the Trinity, and all other doctrines are merely listed briefly in the last clause. The importance of this doctrine is mirrored in the epistles of John, where the center of the faith is acknowledging that Jesus is the Son of God. Those who are against the faith, who are called anti-Christ, deny this (1 John 2:22; 2 John 7). First John is also where the disputed verse about the Trinity occurs (or doesn't occur).

However, the Trinity is established firmly in the Bible even without this verse. It is true that you can't find the words "Trinity" or "three in one" in the Bible, but you also can't find phrases such as "resurrection of the body," "priesthood of all believers," or "communion of the saints." Yet these doctrines are based on the Bible, just as the Trinity is.

Although only a couple of verses have all three members of the Godhead in a single list (2 Cor 13:14; Matt 28:19), there are many others that refer to all three together (especially Luke 3:22; Acts 2:33; 1 Cor 6:11; Gal 4:6; see also John 20:21-22; Acts 1:4-5;

5:3–4; 7:55–56; 10:38; 11:15–17; Rom 5:5–6; 8:3–4, 16–17; 1 Cor 12:4–6; Eph 1:17; 4:4–6; 1 Thess 1:3–5; 2 Thess 2:13–14; Titus 3:4–6; Heb 2:3–4; 9:14; 10:29–30; 1 Pet 1:2; 1 John 3:23–24; 4:13–14; Jude 20–21). Other passages state or imply that the Holy Spirit is God (e.g., Acts 5:3–4; 2 Cor 3:17–18) and speak of Jesus as God (e.g., John 1:1; Acts 10:36; Rom 1:4; Phil 2:6; Col 1:15; 2:9). The New Testament also quotes Old Testament statements about God and applies them to Jesus (e.g., Rom 10:9–13 = Joel 2:32; Phil 2:10 = Isa 45:23). We can even see hints of it in the Old Testament when God says to himself: "Let us …" and "in our image" (Gen 1:26; 3:22; 11:7).

Sadly, the early church was pulled apart by disputes about the Trinity because it is so difficult to square with other important doctrines such as the unity and changelessness of God. Some said that Jesus wasn't ever a real mortal, because God can't die. Others said he completely put aside his godhead while on earth, because he "emptied himself" (Phil 2:7). These disputes were ended by establishing official creedal statements describing Jesus as "fully God" and "fully man." These creeds became almost more important than Bible texts for establishing doctrine.

I do have some concerns about the doctrine of the Trinity as it came to be formulated in the creeds. I don't think we've got it wrong, but it can encourage us to think too simplistically. We don't take into account passages such as Romans 8:9–10, where the Holy Spirit is called both "the Spirit of God" and "the Spirit of Christ" (see also 2 Cor 3:17–18; Gal 4:6; Heb 9:14). Of course, this may merely be different ways to refer to the one Spirit, but it may also imply that our concept of three equal and separate persons is oversimplified. There are likely to be interrelationships in the Godhead that we can't encompass with simple creedal statements.

We don't want to reduce doctrine to slogans because these can be as oversimplified as a politician's sound-bite. But most of us don't want to read long theological explorations of the Trinity either, so we often resort to illustrations, with the result that the Godhead gets shrunk to the size of a three-leaf clover. I may be about to make things worse, because I want to illustrate the Trinity by looking at the atom.

STILL EXPLORING

An atom was considered indivisible for two thousand years until we discovered it is made of three parts: electrons, protons, and neutrons. In a similar way, for a couple of thousand years Jews disseminated the precious truth that there is only one God, until Christ revealed a threefold structure within that Godhead.

In this illustration, we could say that electrons are like the Holy Spirit. They travel as far from the core (in relative terms) as asteroids traveling around the solar system, and their influence extends far outside the atom through electrical and chemical interactions. Protons are perhaps like the Father because they determine the fundamental character of the atom. If the core has six protons, the atom is sooty carbon, but add just one more and it becomes gaseous nitrogen. Neutrons, the third component of atoms, are similar to protons, but a few of them can leave the core without altering the atom's character. For example, carbon-14 and carbon-12 act identically inside our body, even though one is lighter by two neutrons. Jesus is a little like neutrons because he can be separate from the Father, and yet this type of absence does not diminish or change the Godhead.

OK, this is no better than a host of other illustrations because, like them, it breaks down as soon as you start to investigate any detail. However, it does have one advantage: we are still investigating atoms, and we are discovering new complexities. We now know that neutrons and protons are each made of three quarks, and that electrons interact by constantly emitting and absorbing photons; and that's just the start. Now, if we are willing to explore the complexities of atoms, we might also be willing to continue exploring the nature of God. If the Trinity can be compared to an atom, perhaps we should be prepared to explore additional complexities within it. That is, we might continue to dig into Scripture instead of complacently resting on what has already been discovered.

Unlike those who were worried about the removal of the Johannine Comma, we shouldn't expect to encapsulate the Creator of the universe in a handful of theological slogans. The Creator must be at least as complex as his creation. Simple doctrinal statements are good as summaries, as long as we don't fool ourselves into thinking that they accurately represent the complex reality. Doctrines are valuable stepping stones to guide our paths while exploring more about God. He encourages us to find out about him in creation and the Bible. And he has given us firm foundations established by former saints and scholars. These are firm footings that enable us to explore the depths of Scripture more fully.

21

▾

Sacrifice

Jewish animal offerings were killed painlessly, so the concept of a sacrifice implied a costly gift, not suffering. What did Paul and others mean when they compared Jesus' death to a sacrifice?

My teenage daughter returned from a foreign trip and was regaling us with her adventures. She'd described several experiences before hitting us with "And I took part in a ritual slaughter." I decided to remain calm and let her tell me about it.

The group had been helping renovate a school in rural Mongolia, and the villagers wanted to give them a feast to express their thanks. As honored guests, they were invited to share in the slaughter of the goat for their meal. They sat down around an expensive rug with an elder who had a knife and a bowl. He stroked the goat, talked to it quietly until it was calm enough to lie on the rug unrestrained, then put the bowl beside it and made a small incision in its neck. The goat didn't even bleat. It just lay there, being stroked and falling asleep as the bowl filled with blood. Gradually it stopped breathing.

Old Testament sacrifices were very similar to the killing of the goat witnessed by my daughter. Of course, there was still plenty of blood, and they would not have taken place in a quiet gathering—the Temple was a busy place. However, the animals were killed in the same humane way—by slitting their jugular and letting the blood drain out—because this was the only way to make sure that all the blood was removed (Lev 17:11–14).

In contrast, when we think about sacrifice today, we associate it with suffering and horror—ideas that are confirmed in our minds because Jesus' death was so horrific. If "sacrifice" didn't signify the pain and cruelty of Jesus' death, then what does the New Testament mean when it describes Jesus' death as a sacrifice for sin?

NOT SUFFERING BUT A GIFT

Personally, I like to imagine that meat grows inside supermarket packaging because I find the concept of slaughtering animals somewhat horrifying. However, I can see that Jewish sacrifices involved minimal suffering and were in line with other Old Testament laws against animal cruelty (e.g., Exod 23:5, 12; Deut 22:4–7; 25:4). Most animals in the Jewish sacrificial system were killed by the person who brought them. The owner may well have known the animal well—if they were farmers they probably helped deliver it and watched it grow. During the journey to the Temple, they would have kept it away from other animals to make sure it didn't get blemished in any way. The easiest way of doing so was to keep it in their own tents, so it became almost like a pet. The manner in which it died would therefore have been important to them, and later rabbinic law said that if the knife wasn't sharp enough to prevent the animal feeling pain, it wasn't kosher.[1]

So while "sacrifice" makes me think of a victim suffering, an ancient Jewish reader would have regarded it differently: as a gift from the person making the offering. We still use the term "sacrifice" in a similar way when we say, "Giving that will be a real

---

1. See "Shechita," *Wikipedia* (TinyURL.com/WikiShechita).

sacrifice." This concept of a really valuable gift or commitment is how a first-century Jew would have understood the doctrine of Jesus' sacrifice. Even an urban Jew in the first century would not link "sacrifice" with "suffering" because they'd be familiar with the emphasis on the pain-free killing of sacrifices. They were very aware of this because they knew that if the animal they brought suffered pain, their offering was liable to be refused.

Sin offerings were central to Jewish religion—they reminded people to say sorry to God in order to be reconciled to him—so this imagery was an effective way of explaining the significance of Jesus' death. And they were different from other offerings. Most offerings were celebrated with a party: you had to eat the sacrificed animal immediately, so you would invite lots of family and friends to help you. In contrast, sin offerings could only be eaten by priests. By accepting and eating your offering on God's behalf, the priests demonstrated that your relationship with God was healed. That's why Moses became so angry when, on one occasion, the priests didn't eat a sin offering (Lev 10:16–17).

WANTING TO BE RECONCILED

We know that Jesus bore the consequences of our sin (as fore-seen in Isa 53), but we shouldn't confuse that suffering with the Jewish concept of sacrifice. For them, sacrifices represent *recon-ciliation*, not punishment. The word "atonement" was invented by William Tyndale, who couldn't find a way of denoting this concept in English so merged the words "at-one-ment." It indi-cates the reuniting of people or groups who were estranged. Sin—the barrier between God and humanity—was removed by sacrifice, and the visible proof of this was that God came and ate a meal with you. Actually, of course, all you could see was the priests eating your meal, but this was as close as you got to eating with God until Jesus introduced the Eucharist.

Paul elaborates this concept in Colossians 1:20–22: "You were alienated from God and were enemies in your minds because of your evil behavior. But now he has *reconciled* you by Christ's physical body through death." In 2 Corinthians 5:19–21 he defines what kind of sacrifice was needed: "God was *reconciling* the world to himself in Christ, not counting people's sins against them. ... God made him who had no sin to be a sin offering for us, so that in him we might become the righteousness of God" (2 Cor 5:19, 21). The NIV text actually says "to be sin for us," but the translation "to be a sin offering" is in the footnote. It is based on the fact that this Greek word means "sin offering" in the Greek translation of the Old Testament, where it is used more than fifty times. Jesus was our sin offering.

The most important sin offering in the Jewish sacrificial system occurred on the Day of Atonement, when, uniquely, the animal was burned outside the city—a parallel with Jesus, who was crucified outside the city (Heb 13:11–12). This and all the other sin offerings were pointless after Jesus' sacrifice. These sacrifices had *symbolically* reunited sinners with God, but Jesus' death *actually* reunited sinners with God. His sacrifice finally fulfilled the longing of all the people who had brought such offerings over the centuries in order to be reconciled to God.

In Israel's sacrificial system, God didn't require a huge feast— any small offering was sufficient. If you were poor, you could bring a couple of doves or even a small amount of flour; they were equally acceptable for atonement, even for the same sin (see Lev 5:7–13). This showed that the significance of a sin offering wasn't punishment, and the amount didn't relate to the sin like someone paying a fine. The sin offering was a gift—however much you could afford—to show God that you were sorry. God was like the prodigal's father, who longed for any indication, however small, that his son wanted to be reconciled.

THE MOST VALUABLE OFFERING

We lose this precious message when we confuse sacrifice with punishment. Paul explains that Jesus' sacrifice "destroyed the barrier, the dividing wall of hostility, by setting aside in his flesh the law with its commands and regulations" (Eph 2:14-15). Unlike the image of vicarious suffering (which is a separate aspect of Christ's death), the image of sacrifice emphasizes that God wants us back at any cost—even the death of his son. A sacrifice was not made more valuable by making the victim suffer more, because no sacrificial victim was supposed to suffer. A greater sacrifice was made by bringing a more expensive animal such as an ox. God's sacrifice, by which he wanted to reconcile us to himself, was the most valuable offering imaginable.

The language of sacrifice shows that the cross is about a father who longs to gather his lost children, a shepherd who goes looking for stray sheep, and a husband who (like the prophet Hosea) forgives the wife who has strayed—and he is willing to pay whatever it takes. If we put all our emphasis on punishment for sins, it means that we can forget God's grace and forgiveness. No single representation of the cross can convey its full meaning, and attempting to rely on only one explanation will lead us astray. Jesus suffered for us in his death, and his death was a sacrifice—but these are entirely separate aspects of the cross.

For many of us, our personal horror at the concept of animal sacrifice may have made us miss a precious aspect of this portrayal of Jesus' sacrifice and left a huge gap in our theology. Jesus' sacrifice, seen through the eyes of a first-century reader, unveils a glimpse of the depth of God's love. Like the heartfelt plea by a bereft father who longs to reunite with his children, at any cost, God offered to us his own son as an atoning sacrifice—the most costly gift he possessed.

22

▼

Jesus' Punishment for Sin

Talking about God punishing Jesus might give the impression that God is a cruel father. The Bible says that Jesus bore our punishment, but surprisingly it never actually says that God directly punished him.

One of my biggest professional gaffes was when I was on a review board for Steve Chalke's *The Lost Message of Jesus* before publication, and I didn't spot how people might misconstrue one passage. It included one particularly nasty term coined by the Japanese American theologian Rita Nakashima Brock, who compared the crucifixion to "cosmic child abuse."[1] Steve said that he disagreed with this, saying that the crucifixion was *not* like that. But many readers believed he had invented the phrase (because he didn't cite the source), so they thought Steve gave tacit support to this concept despite his expressed disagreement. Consequently, his book caused a huge controversy among UK evangelicals on a similar seismic scale to Rob Bell's book *Love Wins* in the US.

For the record I'd like to say that the crucifixion isn't at all, in any way, remotely, no way, never, ever to be regarded like that! Sometimes, though, when I preach about the cross, a listener

---

1. The phrase comes from *Journeys by Heart: A Christology of Erotic Power* (New York: Crossroad, 1988), 56.

might *think* that's what I'm saying—and I suspect this is why I react so strongly against this ghastly phrase. I have often preached things such as: "My sins were wiped away when God poured the agonies of my punishment onto Jesus." This implies that God himself was punishing Jesus with one of the cruelest forms of torture ever invented. But when I think about it, I realize that I'm in danger of portraying God as though he were uglier than some of the amoral Greek and Roman gods. I'm presenting the holy God as a perpetrator of parental cruelty, which is rightly regarded as revolting and illegal in every civilized society.

I would defend myself by saying we have to be true to what the Bible says. It tells us that God is rightly angry at sin and if we don't repent, we will face his wrath (John 3:36; Rom 2:5, 8; 3:5; Eph 5:6; Col 3:6; Rev 6:16–17). It also says that Jesus saves us from that wrath (Rom 5:9; 1 Thess 1:10; 5:9) and that our salvation from that wrath came by means of Jesus' suffering (Rom 4:25; 1 Pet 2:21–24; Isa 53:4–5) as well as by his death. It is therefore easy to understand how many of us have jumped to the obvious conclusion that God poured his wrath on Jesus by punishing him in our place—in fact it is a very common teaching. However, none of the authors of the Bible actually described salvation in this way.

HOW THE BIBLE SAYS IT

I was very surprised when I did a careful search for supporting Bible texts, and I asked a group of other Bible enthusiasts to look too. I wanted to find a place in the Bible that says or predicts that God punished Jesus for our sins. Of course, there are places that speak about Jesus being "despised," "stricken" (i.e., being struck with something), "crushed," "pierced," "condemned," "cursed," and "insulted" (Isa 53:3–5; Gal 3:13; 1 Pet 2:23)—but we are never told that this was done by God! It took me a long time to accept that there was no text in support of this idea. Some others in the group also refused to believe that there wasn't a text, even though none had been found.

This doesn't necessarily mean that it isn't true that God punished Jesus for our sins, but it does mean that we should take care how forcefully we state the conclusion. We can still preach that "God punished Jesus for our sins," but we should be aware that we have extrapolated this from the Bible, and it is something that the Bible itself never says. On the other hand, if the Bible can describe God's salvation in so many places without ever saying that God punished his son, then perhaps we also should avoid stating it this way.

The reason we like to speak about God punishing Jesus is that this view of the cross helps to explain why Jesus had to suffer so terribly, and it helps us understand how a righteous God deals with sin. However, like all images or metaphors, not every detail fits perfectly with the full meaning of the crucifixion. As soon as we assume that God himself punished or poured suffering onto Jesus, we fall into problems. John Stott made this clear when he warned against using a "crude construction" in which we portray the cross as "a sacrifice to appease an angry God, or ... a legal transaction in which an innocent victim was made to pay the penalty for the crimes of others."[2] According to Stott, this is "a caricature" of the true doctrine of penal substitution.

The term "penal substitution"—the idea that Jesus endured the penalty for our sins on our behalf—is not problematic. This phrase sums up perfectly what we know from the Bible: that Jesus suffered in order to save us, and because he suffered, we won't face God's wrath. That is, because of Jesus' substitutionary

---

2. John Stott, *The Cross of Christ* (Downers Grove, IL: InterVarsity Press, 1986), 172. Stott is quoting this "caricature" from William Neil (TinyURL.com/StottCrossOfChrist).

sacrifice, we won't suffer the penalty of God's wrath—hence "penal substitution." The problem lies in the way that we present this. As Stott warned, we should avoid saying something that the Bible doesn't say; and it doesn't say that God punished Jesus instead of us.

The main Bible passage concerning penal substitution is Isaiah 53, where a servant of God on whom he has "laid … the iniquity of us all" is described as suffering on behalf of sinners. This is applied to Jesus in various places (especially John 12:38; Acts 8:32–33; Rom 4:25; 1 Pet 2:21–25). These passages emphasize the rejection and suffering of Jesus, but none of them state that God himself was the source of his suffering. One verse comes extremely close to saying this but steps back from doing so. Isaiah 53:10 says that the suffering heaped on this servant was "the Lord's will." This implies that God permitted it, though putting it like this deliberately avoids saying that God himself did it. The Hebrew may imply God's involvement a little more strongly, because it could be translated either "the Lord wished to crush him" or "the Lord wished him to be crushed." The technical reason for this ambiguity lies in the grammatical form: a *piel* infinitive. The only other occurrence of this form of this verb is in the phrase "to crush underfoot all prisoners." In that instance it says God does *not* will it (Lam 3:34), and it is clearly not done *by* God in that case. This doesn't mean we can be certain which way to translate Isaiah 53:10, but it shows that it may well mean "the Lord wished him to be crushed"—that is, by someone else. The significance of this is not that we aren't sure, but that the text carefully avoids stating that God was directly punishing him.

We might, of course, conclude that God, who is in charge of all things, was acting through the Jews and Romans who executed Jesus, because we know from Isaiah 53:10 that it *was* God's will. However, this introduces new difficulties. If we conclude that all the evil that humans do (such as killing Christ) is by the direct control of God, it is tantamount to saying that God is also directing and controlling us when we sin. This means that if God was directly punishing Jesus through his executioners, then he is also directly causing the sins for which Jesus was punished! The Bible avoids saying anything that implies this, so perhaps we should too.

Instead, the Bible simply informs us that Jesus suffered the consequence of sin and "the curse of the law" (Gal 3:13–14), and that his suffering saves us from God's wrath (Rom 5:9; 1 Thess 1:10; 5:9). We never read that God himself turned his wrath or punishment or curse on Jesus. Of course, we can choose to infer something that is not stated in the text. We can theorize that God punished Jesus just as he would have punished us, which is why we no longer face that punishment—but we have to real-ize what we are doing: we are filling in a detail that the Bible is silent about.

OTHER MODELS OF THE CROSS

This "punishment" imagery isn't the only way that the Bible attempts to explain the crucifixion to us. We are also told that Jesus "redeemed" us (i.e., ransomed us back from slavery or kidnapping, e.g., Mark 10:45); he "reconciled" us (i.e., repaired our broken relationship with God, e.g., Rom 5:10); he "abolished the law" (Eph 2:14–15); and he defeated demonic forces at the cross (e.g., Col 2:14–15). These are all valid and useful images and explanations of what happened at the crucifixion, but none of them are adequate by themselves—we need them all in order to understand the cross.

The cross-as-punishment image may be useful to present the gospel as a solution to sin in cases where we want to avoid mentioning a personal devil. The "redemption" or "ransom"

images imply that we were captured by an enemy; "reconciliation" implies we were previously allied with an enemy; and
"abolishing the law" was accomplished by "triumphing over"
the enemy. All of these imply the existence of the devil, which
could make the gospel less believable for those non-Christians
who don't think Satan exists. This means that the gospel can
be presented in a way that is easier to understand for them. On
the other hand, the current generation is thoroughly engaged
with stories of conflict against strange forces, and this may be
the right time to describe the cross in a way that the Bible often
does—as a battle against evil.

We know that all of these images are incomplete; none of
them are a full explanation of what happened at the cross. We
can see that they are incomplete when we try to investigate
details that aren't actually explored in Scripture—because they
start to become inconsistent. For example, if the enemy was
defeated, then why pay any ransom money? If the law was abolished, then why was any punishment required? These questions
are, of course, nonsensical. They are like asking: Is an electron
a particle or a wave? The answer is that both images of an electron are correct, but neither is adequate. The realities of both
the cross and atomic physics are more complex than the images
we use to describe them. Each of these scriptural images of the
cross gives us only partial insights into a reality our minds can't
comprehend fully.

Isaiah 53 is a precious insight into the crucifixion. It tells us
that Jesus' suffering was real human agony. It helps us understand the dereliction and sense of abandonment behind his cry,
"My God, my God, why have you forsaken me?" Through it, we
can see his love for us. It is also theologically important because
it shows that his suffering was on our behalf and that it dealt
with our sin. However, when we infer from this that Jesus was

being punished directly by God, we should be aware that we are concluding something that Scripture itself doesn't state and appears to be careful to avoid.

So how do we understand the cross? I believe that J. I. Packer gave us the solution: "The mystery of God is more than any one model, even the best, can express."[3] The Bible gives us many ways to comprehend the crucifixion, and we need them all—including that Jesus suffered the penalty for our sins. Each of them helps us to fathom a little more about God's love and mercy, which he enacted on our behalf though the suffering of his Son.

3. J. I. Packer, "What Did the Cross Achieve?" (TinyURL.com/PackerCross).

23

▼

Redemption

Payments to redeem a kidnap victim or to buy a slave are strange images for salvation, but in Bible times these concepts were regarded very differently from how we think about them today.

I was worried when my daughter said her new friend kidnaps people for a living. He was large, but he appeared to be gentle. It turned out that his firm is hired to perform abductions—including hooding and moderate violence—on unsuspecting trainees being sent to dangerous environments. This is necessary, because kidnapping and ransom is big business for the pirates and terrorists who use it as a profitable source of income, and these workers need to know what to expect and how to react to minimize danger to themselves.

Kidnapping for ransom is by no means a new activity. One reason Jews tolerated Herod the Great was his defeat of bandits during his early reign, but by the first century AD others had filled the gap. One result was that when Jesus attended a wedding, he would be likely to hear a vow that no modern groom needs to make: "If you are kidnapped, I will ransom you." It was a relatively new part of the marriage ceremony, necessitated by the real threat of kidnapping by vicious bandits. If a woman was kidnapped and held even for more than a few minutes, it was assumed she'd been violated. The vow was necessary because a pious man might feel obligated to live separately from her now that she was "defiled," so he might be tempted not to ransom her unless he had made this pledge.[1]

Jesus referred to himself as a ransom (in Mark 10:44), but some early theologians disliked this image. I think they took it too literally. They wanted to know to whom the money was paid, and they argued, reasonably, that if the payment had been to Satan, then God was giving in to his unjust demands. To counteract this, Saint Anselm in the eleventh century referred to the payment as a "fine"—that is, a penalty or punishment for our sins. Therefore, there was a just reason why payment could be demanded in order to free sinners. However, this image, like the image of ransom, can also be taken too literally, because it raises the question: Who demanded the fine—Satan? We can solve this absurdity by looking at what ransom and redemption meant in the Bible.

PAYING A RANSOM

In Old Testament law, you were required to either sacrifice or "redeem" every firstborn son or animal—that is, buy them back from God (Num 18:15–16). Since people could not be sacrificed, they *had* to be redeemed.

This law originated from the time when Israel escaped Egypt and God protected the firstborn Israelite males from the final terrible plague that killed the firstborn of the Egyptians. Because God had spared them, they were regarded in some way as belonging to him. But instead of paying money to the Tabernacle for all the firstborn who came out of Egypt, the men of the tribe of Levi were given to God for religious service. They

---

1. See Papyri Yadin 10 in my "Aramaic Marriage and Divorce Papyri," *Tyndale Bulletin* 52 (2001): 225–43 (TinyURL.com/JewishMarriageContracts).

were almost the same in number as the firstborn males who had been saved, so only the difference had to be paid in shekels (see Num 3).

When Jesus called himself a ransom, he seemed to compare and contrast himself to these Levites. Like the Levites, he gave his life (including his death) in service to God and humanity, as a ransom. But, whereas each Levite could redeem only one firstborn, Jesus is a ransom for "many"—that is, for everyone who repents.

The Old Testament Hebrew doesn't actually refer to these Levites as a "ransom"—that word is reserved for the money payment itself. However, by New Testament times, Jews were used to the concept that a person could be a ransom payment. The Septuagint (the Jews' Greek translation of the Old Testament) does call the Levites "a ransom" for Israel (Num 3:12), using the same word that was normally reserved for "money payments." Jesus was making the point that his life was so valuable that the exchange rate wasn't one for one (as it was with the Levites); his single life could redeem everyone.

Paul used a different image of a payment to explain the cross. He likened salvation to the redemption loophole that enabled a Greek or Roman slave to get himself released. The slave could save up money and pay it to a temple, so that the god would then purchase him with that money. This meant that, legally, he now belonged to that god, so he owed that god his allegiance. A large wall still standing at the shrine at Delphi in Greece records the names of many slaves who were redeemed in this way. Paul said that Christians should apply the same rule to themselves; they were bought from slavery to sin, so they should now regard themselves as belonging to God (1 Cor 6:19-20; 7:22-23). He used this image to show that Christians should live completely for God, because their freedom was bought by Christ.

Some Christians conclude that the redemption imagery in the Bible indicates that God has to obey "justice"—rather like a modern ruler has to obey the law. But this speculation about the literal meaning of "ransom" implies something that Scripture does not: that God is constrained by some kind of law that is higher than God himself. It is as if this law demands punishment for sin or the payment of a fine, and God has to obey it. It is very difficult to believe in this kind of law and also God's sovereignty. But even if there is such a law, we should be aware that it is not what the original readers would have envisioned when redemption was mentioned.

FURTHER IMAGES OF SALVATION

When thinking about how salvation works, it's important to remind ourselves that the descriptions the Bible gives us are merely *images*—none are a complete explanation—and we should take care when trying to interpret them further than we are invited to by Scripture. For example, while the Bible portrays Satan as Jesus' opponent, it does not say that Satan received any ransom payment. Satan can, perhaps, be regarded as our former slave master, but the Bible does not say that Jesus bought us back from him.

When first-century readers considered redemption by Jesus, they would have thought about being rescued from kidnapping (possibly by Satan), being redeemed as a firstborn, or being freed from slavery to sin or Satan so that we are now owned by God. Another glorious way that Paul describes salvation at the cross uses the image of a battleground where Jesus defeated Satan and released many "captives" (Col 2:14–15; Eph 4:8–9). This complements the image of release from captivity or slavery that is illustrated by the concept of redemption.

While the images of paying fines may emphasize God's justice, the images of paying a ransom emphasize God's love. Both are true: God is a severe judge whose justice was balanced by Jesus' self-sacrifice and also a loving Father who sent his best warrior to defeat his enemy. Scripture describes our salvation using many different images, because the work of the cross is simply too big to be understood through one image alone. "Ransomed," "redeemed," and "rescued" are all aspects of God's wonderful salvation plan, through which we can catch a glimpse of the breadth and depth of his love for us.

24

▼

New Life

What happens when we become a Christian? The images of a new birth and adoption might imply we have no role in this, but what did they mean in Bible times?

Watching your child being born is one of the most trans-forming events someone can have in life. You not only instantly become a parent, but when you first see that crumpled face you can immediately fall in love. You can't imagine that little bundle of perfection ever being a disappointment to you. Well, that's the theory, anyway! We all grow up with regrets and mistakes, disappointing our parents and ourselves. That's one reason why we love the idea of being "born again"—of having a second chance at life. A *new* life in Christ is at the heart of the gospel.

The interesting thing is that when Jesus described this new life to the Pharisee Nicodemus, he probably wasn't saying "You must be born *again*" (John 3:7) but instead "You must be born *from above*." The confusion is because these two phrases are identical in Greek: the word *anōthen* can mean either "again" or "above" (as in v. 31). This ambiguity is similar to the English phrase "from the top." Usually it means "from above," but we can also use it in the sense of "again"—for instance, a choir master saying: "Let's sing it from the top." English Bibles translate Jesus saying, "You must be born again" rather than "from above" because that's the only way to make sense of how Nicodemus responds. He clearly interpreted it this way because he complains that no one can leave a womb twice (v. 4).[1]

REBORN

Even though Jesus had a different emphasis, it doesn't mean we should reject the idea of being born again; it is still an appropriate—and powerful—way of expressing God's invitation to a new life. And when Nicodemus misunderstood his words, Jesus didn't reject this meaning. Instead, he gently moved him on toward what he *did* want to emphasize: that we need to be born from above, that is, "born of the Spirit" (John 3:8). Jesus had to drum this in by repeating it several times in different ways: born not just by the waters of physical birth but also of the Spirit (v. 5); born not just of flesh but also of Spirit (v. 6); born not just in an "earthly" way but in a "heavenly" way (v. 12). I guess Nicodemus understood it eventually, but it is harder for us because English doesn't have the same ambiguity. In the end, being born of the Spirit as well as of the flesh is, of course, a second birth, so Nicodemus didn't really get it wrong—he just missed the most precious bit of Jesus' message.

Throughout John's Gospel, Jesus' message that you must be born of the Spirit continues with teaching such as "the Spirit gives life; the flesh counts for nothing" (6:63); "'rivers of living water will flow from within them.' By this he meant the Spirit" (7:38–39); "the Spirit of truth ... lives with you and will be in you" (14:17); and just before Jesus ascended to heaven, "he breathed on

---

1. Interestingly, this implies that Jesus' conversation with Nicodemus was in Greek—the language of religious debate among Romans. Jewish scholars didn't debate in everyday Aramaic, but they normally preferred to use Hebrew.

them and said, 'Receive the Holy Spirit'" (20:22). In other Gospels the same message is conveyed in terms of baptism of the Spirit (Matt 3:11 = Mark 1:8 = Luke 3:16; Acts 1:5).

Peter refers to being reborn (1 Pet 1:23), but at first it looks as though this message is entirely dropped by Paul. Of course, it isn't absent, but he teaches it using different imagery. Instead of referring to new birth in the Spirit, Paul talks about new creation (2 Cor 5:17; Gal 6:15; Eph 4:23-24; Col 3:10) and about new life after baptism (Rom 6:4).

REHOMED

Paul also uses another image that is close to the idea of a second birth: he speaks of adoption, saying that we were adopted into God's family (Gal 4:4-7; Rom 8:15-17). Jews would not have had a good understanding of adoption, but Romans practiced it widely, so the image worked really well. Although a childless Roman couple could obtain an unwanted baby, it was more common to adopt a teenager. This was regarded as preferable to adopting a young child because infant mortality was so high. Also, by adopting a young adult you could be sure of their character, whereas a baby might grow up to be a stupid or careless heir. Most importantly, Romans wanted to adopt someone old enough to give personal assurances that they were willing to carry on the traditions and responsibilities of the family. A nice example of this is in the story of Ben Hur, who was adopted as the son of a rich, childless man who was impressed by his character.

This Roman practice of adoption is a wonderful picture of what it is like to become a Christian, and Paul uses the image to point out that we become children of God and heirs of the kingdom. However, as modern readers, we tend to miss a very important aspect of Roman adoption that also applies to the process of salvation: God invites us into his family, but that adoption only occurs when we accept his invitation by agreeing to follow the lifestyle and aims of his family.

Jews didn't practice that kind of adoption, so Jesus used a different image to teach them—that of being born into God's family by a second birth from above (John 3:3–7). For Jews, the all-important birth was your first one: if your mother was Jewish, then so were you—and they believed that all Jews were saved. But Jesus said your earthly birth wasn't as important as the second birth that occurs when you invite the Holy Spirit to make you completely new again.

A NEW START

Neither Jesus' illustration of birth from above nor Paul's illustration of adoption would have made people think about infants, but our minds *are* drawn that way. And because babies can't choose their parents—or anything else—we might conclude that we have no role in becoming Christians. So it feels as if salvation is something that happens to us outside our control, and we can't *choose* to make God our Father. But Paul's image of adoption suggests that we do have at least a partial role. God, who wants to adopt us, has to make the first move, but we, like Roman teenagers or adults, have to decide to accept the responsibilities and consequences of joining his family. The new birth "from above" similarly requires that we accept the indwelling of the Holy Spirit not just as a passive presence but as a transforming influence. Our lives experience a fresh start—as a new creation—but this doesn't start till we invite the Holy Spirit to transform us. All this is symbolized by the cleansing of baptism, which is performed when someone decides to be baptized or personally confirms their infant baptism.

We have been given a wonderful array of images of what happens when someone becomes a Christian—baptism, new birth, adoption, new creation—and some work better in one culture than another: baptism was a Jewish practice, and adoption was a familiar concept to Romans. These images also emphasize different aspects of salvation, but they all have common themes such as a new start and welcoming in the Holy Spirit. None of them convey the whole truth, of course, but together they have given us a very real insight into God's wonderful work of regeneration.

25

▼

Repentance

In Jewish theology we must ask forgiveness from those we have hurt before God will accept our repentance. This explains how repentance works in the Bible and why God demands it before forgiving us.

Why doesn't God just forgive our sins without our needing to repent and ask his forgiveness? After all, Jesus has paid for them through his death on the cross. Wouldn't more people come into the kingdom without this negative aspect—especially those who are too proud to ask for forgiveness?

Repentance is easy to ignore because it is mentioned relatively little in the Bible. This is for the same reason that the Bible doesn't spend time giving proofs for God's existence: nobody disputed it in those times. There were hardly any atheists, and everyone understood that a moral God required repentance.

In fact, ordinary Jews understood one aspect of repentance better than most Christian theologians. We tend to emphasize that we should repent to God and ask him for forgiveness, but Jews know that before repenting to God, we should repent to those whom we have hurt and ask for *their* forgiveness. On the annual Day of Atonement (a day devoted to repentance), they followed an ancient Jewish rule: "For transgressions between a man and God, the Day of Atonement atones. But for transgressions between a man and his fellow, the Day of Atonement does not atone, until he seeks pardon from his fellow."[1] If we understood this better, we'd see why repentance is not just an obligation but essential for our relationships with God and other people.

REPENTANCE IS URGENT

Jesus' teaching agrees with this traditional Jewish teaching, though he thought that repenting to someone you had hurt was too important to wait until the Day of Atonement. In fact, it was even more urgent than worshiping God: "If you are offering your gift at the altar and there remember that your brother or sister has something against you, leave your gift there in front of the altar. First go and be reconciled to them; then come and offer your gift" (Matt 5:23–24). God doesn't want you to repent to him until you've repented to others.

It seems that we've forgotten this important doctrine today. Perhaps one reason is that we misunderstand Psalm 51, where David is confessing his adultery with Bathsheba. He says to God: "Against you, you only, have I sinned and done what is evil in your sight" (v. 4). We realize that David had also sinned against Bathsheba and against her husband, whom he had sent to the front line knowing he'd be killed, and yet David seemed to think he had only sinned against God. So we conclude that sins against God are much more important than sins against people and that repenting to people is unimportant compared with repenting to God. But this is backwards in the light of the traditional Jewish teaching that you should *first* repent to people you have sinned against. We should instead conclude that David wouldn't have dared ask for God's forgiveness if he had not already begged forgiveness from Bathsheba. If he had not done this, God would know that he wasn't yet truly repentant.

---

1. Mishnah Yoma 8:9 (TinyURL.com/MishnahRepent).

On the Day of Atonement all Jews repented to God (preferably with tears), begging him to forgive them for the past year's sins. But they knew that God wouldn't listen unless they'd already tried equally hard to be forgiven by the people they'd wronged. Paradoxically, this gave a powerful weapon to those whose forgiveness was being sought, because they could withhold this from the person who was now pleading for it. So Jesus, who knows the nastiness of the human heart, emphasized the flip side, saying that you *must* forgive those who come to you repenting for the wrong they did to you. To further press this point home, he said that if you don't forgive that person, then God won't forgive you for your wrongs. He came back to this many times and even included it in his template for daily prayer (Matt 6:12, 14; 18:15-35; Luke 6:37; 11:4; 17:3-4).

SAY SORRY TO EACH OTHER

The loss of this aspect of the doctrine of repentance—that we should ask forgiveness from people first—explains some of our misunderstandings about God's forgiveness. When people ask why God doesn't simply forgive our sin instead of waiting for us to repent, we're inclined to answer: God cannot forgive sin until we have accepted that Jesus has paid for our sins, as a gift. This is true, but it can give the impression that God is a bureaucrat waiting for a transaction to be carried out properly. We get a much better understanding of why he requires our repentance if we consider the way in which Jesus' parables illustrate it as forgiveness between humans.

Imagine you regularly give a friend a lift in your car, and you notice that your collection of parking-meter coins often diminishes during these trips. One day you try to prompt him to admit he's helping himself by saying, "That's funny, I thought I had more coins than that." But your friend simply shrugs and says nothing. From then on, there's a barrier between the two of you: you don't trust him, and he feels guilty. If only he'd say: "I'm sorry—I sometimes take a few coins for the coffee machine." Then you'd probably say something like: "That's fine—but please ask in the future," and it would all be over; your relationship would be back to normal. Until that happens, however, an invisible wall separates you.

Now we see why God can't just forgive us without our repentance; there's an invisible wall—a barrier of sin between us. He wants a relationship with us, but a broken relationship can't be fixed by only one side. It isn't that God is like a legalistic accountant who can't ignore a debt; and God isn't subject to some kind of law of sin that he can't circumvent. The reason he can't simply ignore our sin is that it has broken our relationship, and both parties need to fix this. God has already done his part: he has sent his Son to deal with the consequences of sin and has offered to forgive us. But unless we do our part—unless we repent—it wouldn't be a relationship; it would be merely a transaction.

Seen this way, the call to repentance tells us that God wants to be our Father, rather than our judge. Of course, if we don't repent, we will end up being judged by him for those unforgiven sins, but he doesn't want it to come to that. Actually, he wants something else: he wants to restore a loving friendship. And repentance is the missing ingredient for healing our broken relationship. We teach children "Just say sorry and mean it," and in the end the gospel comes down to the same thing.

26

▼

Justification and Good Works

No official Christian or Jewish theology ever taught that heaven is a reward for a good life—they all emphasize God's grace. So why did Paul bother to preach against salvation by works?

When I started my doctorate on the rabbis of New Testament times, I found that the area of rabbinic studies was suddenly regarded with suspicion by many Christians. A rabbinic scholar, E. P. Sanders, had just published *Paul and Palestinian Judaism* and was at the center of what many regard as a modern heresy: the "new perspective" on Paul. This cast doubt on what Paul meant when he said salvation is by faith and not based on works.

For centuries, Paul's teaching of justification by faith had been assumed to be correcting a Jewish doctrine of "salvation by works." However, Sanders pointed out that Jews in New Testament times did not believe in salvation by works any more than they do now. There were plenty of regulations to keep, just as there were for Christians (Sunday/Sabbath observance, baptism/circumcision, church/synagogue services, various festivals and fasts, etc.), but neither Christians nor Jews thought they would qualify for heaven by living a good life. They all expected to fall short of God's standard, so they relied on his mercy and forgiveness when they repented. Jews even had a special festival—the Day of Atonement—to help them remember anything they may have neglected to repent of. So where did we get the idea that Jews thought they were saved by works?

ALL ISRAEL WILL BE SAVED

Many people outside the church today believe that a place in heaven is earned—perhaps through regularly carrying out certain religious observances, leading a moral life, or simply by being kind and helpful to others. All Christian churches reject this idea—including Catholics, as it says in the Catholic catechism: "Our justification comes from the grace of God. Grace is favor, the free and undeserved help that God gives us to respond to his call to become children of God, adoptive sons, partakers of the divine nature and of eternal life."[1] Of course, "grace" for some Catholics may include the sacraments, but these aren't "good works." Nevertheless, despite what their various churches teach, many Christians still believe that God's salvation is based on living a good life. Perhaps it's no wonder that people outside the church mistakenly think that various kinds of churches teach this doctrine. And in much the same way there has been, until recently, a belief that Jews relied on the good works of keeping the commandments for their salvation.

But Paul knew what Jews really believed—he had so recently been an exemplary practicing Jew himself. So why did he preach against salvation by works as if this were a Jewish doctrine? He said, for example: "No one will be declared righteous in God's sight by the works of the law; rather, through the law we become conscious of our sin" (Rom 3:20); and "The people of Israel, who pursued the law as the way of righteousness, have not attained

---

1. Catechism of the Catholic Church 1996 (TinyURL.com/CatholicGrace).

their goal. Why not? Because they pursued it not by faith but as if it were by works" (Rom 9:31-32).

These verses seem to imply that Jews thought they were gaining salvation by righteous obedience of the law, and only those who succeeded would go to heaven. However, in the time of Jesus they believed that *all* Jews were elect—they were all going to heaven, and the unelect Gentiles were going to hell. The slogan was "All Israel will be saved." Paul clearly disagreed with this because he tried hard to convert Jews, and he affirmed that Gentiles who trusted in Christ were going to heaven. But in what appears to be something of a contradiction, he also quoted the slogan: "All Israel will be saved" (Rom 11:26).

He does so at the end of three chapters in which he explains how this will happen—and many books have been written trying to unravel what he meant. Probably it was one of two things. First, he may have been saying that "all of the *true* Israel will be saved"—that is, all Jewish Christians plus Gentile Christians who are all "grafted in" to the root, which is the elect Israel (see Rom 11:22-24). Or, second, he may have meant that the Jews were going through a time of disobedience, but when that ended (probably at the return of Christ), they would all repent and be saved (see Rom 11:28-32; Zech 12:10). Paul may well have intended this not to be entirely clear because he ends the section with praise for the God of unfathomable mysteries (Rom 11:33-36).

This leaves us with the same question: Why did Paul imply that Jews thought they'd be saved through "works of the law" when they actually taught that "all Israel will be saved"? The situation becomes clearer when we see that although they *did* say that all Jews will be saved (in Mishnah Sanhedrin 10:1), they also had a long list of Jews who were exceptions. In the first century this list comprised only seven named individuals (such as Ahab and Balaam—see Mishnah Sanhedrin 10:2), but it also included anyone who denied core beliefs, including the physical resurrection of believers and the divine inspiration of the books of Moses. Later they added large groups such as the entire wilderness generation, because they didn't have the faith to enter the promised land, and the generation sent into exile. At the start of the second century, when Rabbi Akiva wanted to add everyone in the ten lost tribes of Israel to this list, another influential rabbi, Eliezer ben Hyrcanus, had had enough and objected. He was a conservative rabbi who normally defended the traditions from the first century, so he still believed that "all Israel will be saved" and was convinced this included the ten tribes (Mishnah Sanhedrin 10:3).

EXCLUDED FROM HEAVEN

The Israelites whom these rabbis wanted to exclude from heaven were individuals who didn't believe key doctrines and the generations who didn't have enough faith in God. So they weren't refused salvation for failing to observe the works of the law, but for failing to have faith in God and the Bible's teachings. This means that Christians and Jews should have been on the same page with regard to salvation: it was based on faith in God and repentance for sin. The important difference between Jews and Christians wasn't the matter of good works but the significance of Jesus.

So what did Jews think about the commandments? Their writings indicate that they were extremely keen to keep every law. Every morning they recited the Shema, which includes the words "You will remember all the commands of the Lord, that you may obey them. ... You will remember to obey all my commands. ... These commandments that I give you. ... So if you faithfully obey the commands I am giving you today ..." (from Deut 6:4–9, 11:13–21; Num 15:37–41). Jews certainly wanted to obey the law. In fact they took great pleasure in it. We can see the attitude of an average Jew in a lovely parable told to illustrate the "law of the forgotten sheaf"—a clump of wheat or barley that was accidentally overlooked when the rest was harvested. The law said that rather than going back to harvest the sheaf, you should generously let the poor help themselves to it (Deut 24:19). The parable says:

> A certain pious man forgot a sheaf in the middle of his field. He said to his son, "Go and offer two bullocks on my behalf, for a burnt offering and a peace offering." His son said to him, "Father, why are you more joyful at fulfilling this one commandment than all the other commandments in Torah?" He said to him, "The Lord gave us all the commands in Torah to obey intentionally, but he only gave us this one to obey accidentally." (Tosefta Peah 3:8)

When the farmer notices the forgotten sheaf he is overjoyed because he can now obey a law he couldn't obey deliberately. This law could only be obeyed by accident because you had to unintentionally forget the sheaf and then be generous. The farmer is so happy to be able to obey this law that he sends a huge offering to the Temple in thanks—the equivalent of donating two Mercedes for church ministry. We can see that for Jews, obeying the law wasn't so they could get to heaven but because it gave them joy. For the farmer, getting the opportunity to obey this law was like finding a missing stamp for his collection. So the rabbis didn't teach that salvation is based on obeying the law, either here or anywhere else.

THE WORKS OF THE LAW

We are still not sure why Paul suggests that some Jews aimed to be "declared righteous in God's sight by the works of the law" (Rom 3:20), but there are three main possibilities. First, "the works of the law" may refer to a narrow group of laws that defined what it was to be a Jew—Sabbath, circumcision, and food laws—so keeping these made you into an Israelite, and all such Israelites would be saved.

Second, "the law" may refer to the whole legal system of the Torah—the books of Moses or Law, including all the festivals, Day of Atonement, and so on—so Paul was warning them against putting their trust in this system, rather than in Jesus.

The third possibility (which I favor) is that Paul was talking about a group of Jews who really did rely on their own obedience of the law for their personal salvation. It is likely that the Jews living in the Dead Sea community believed this, because they excluded anyone who didn't keep all the rules according to their particular interpretations, and they regarded themselves as the "true Israel" who would be saved. Presumably other groups thought in a similar way, and there is evidence in the New Testament that one such group existed right inside the early church.

Paul referred to them as "the circumcision group" because they taught that Gentile Christians had to keep Jewish laws and even be circumcised in order to be saved (Gal 2:12-14). In Acts we find them present at two major meetings of the Jerusalem church leadership, where they are very vocal (Acts 11:2; 15:5). In the letter to the Galatians, Paul was especially concerned about the influence they might have on the believers: "Those people are zealous to win you over, but for no good" (4:17); "Stand firm, then, and do not let yourselves ... be circumcised" (5:1-2); "As for those agitators, I wish they would go the whole way and emasculate themselves!" (5:12). As we can see from his intemperate language, Paul was extremely concerned and antagonized by this group.

It may seem strange that we are still puzzling about what the Jews really believed about salvation by works after so many centuries. The problem is that the Jewish world of the first century was almost as varied as the church of our century, but only a few of those factions left any writings to tell us what they believed. So we know what some groups believed, but many we know little about. It seems that this small group who joined the church may have had a very loud voice and that their teaching was something that Paul was really up against. When some of them became Christians, they were certainly influential in the church, in a bad way. So Paul's teaching against salvation by works was directed against this group's persistent campaigning within the church and not against Judaism in general.

Jesus' longest recorded prayer is for the unity of believers (John 17:11, 21), perhaps because he knew what would soon happen and continue to happen. At the earliest opportunity, people tried to carve out their own little empire and sphere of influence within the church, and this continues to our day. Just as Paul was vigilant in his mission not to let a powerful pressure group undermine the incredible doctrine of justification by faith, we need to be on guard not just against the influence of the outside world, but the potential for even very small groups within the church to lead us astray from the truths of the gospel.

27

▾

Saving Faith

The Greek word pistis *has a broad meaning, so it can be translated as "faith," "trust," or "belief." What do they each mean? And which one do we need for salvation?*

The cartoonist Charles Schulz, who created Peanuts, was a keen Christian. One Christmas he featured Lucy telling her little brother Linus, "Santa Claus stops at every house in the whole world, and he climbs down every chimney, and leaves a present for every boy and every girl!" Linus thinks for a moment, saying, "That's hard to believe ... that's awfully hard to believe ..." Then he raises his fist in determination and shouts, "But I believe it!!!"

Some Christians think they need this Linus-style faith—they are saved by believing something with enough conviction. But in the Bible, the faith that saves us is completely different. Actually, the Greek word for faith, *pistis*, means three things, so most English Bibles use three different words when translating it: "belief," "faith," and "trust." These represent three distinct concepts. We *believe a statement*, such as "Jesus died for everyone"; we *have faith in an ability or institution*, such as the ability of Jesus to remove our sins or in the teaching of the church; and we *trust a person*, such as Jesus. We use the same three concepts at a more mundane level when we are invited to sit on an antique chair. We may *believe* that old wood doesn't weaken, so we *have faith* in the ability of the old chair to support our weight. Or we could simply *trust* the person who invited us to sit.

Put like this, they sound very similar, but there are big differences between them.

BELIEF IN A FACT

Belief is the gap between evidence and knowledge. Generally the more evidence you have, the less belief you need. Early Old Testament believers had only the evidence of their own spiritual discernment, and later they had the stories of events such as the exodus. We are more fortunate because we have the life of Jesus—his life and death are facts acknowledged by all reputable historians. But of course historians don't agree on the resurrection, because extraordinary events require extraordinary amounts of evidence, and there isn't anything more extraordinary than a three-day-old corpse reviving itself. So we have to add some belief to the equation.

But James said that we need more than belief. Writing to believers who were proud that they believed in God, he said he wasn't impressed: "Show me your faith without deeds, and I will show you my faith by my deeds" (Jas 2:18). This is a salutary reminder that faith doesn't save us if it doesn't transform us. Faith is not merely a matter of assenting to a set of beliefs. To make sure that his readers had got the point, James then said something startling: "You believe that there is one God. Good! Even the demons believe that—and shudder" (v. 19).

Clearly, demons aren't saved by believing there is one God. But they certainly know who and what God is. They believe there is only one God, just as we believe there is only one sun in our solar system.

The church has gradually emphasized faith as an assent to a set of beliefs because theological disputes have led to the creation of longer and more detailed statements of doctrine. The ancient creeds have been supplemented by statements about evolution, predestination, tribulation, gender, tongues, transubstantiation, and many other doctrines that divide us into multitudinous denominational groups. Most of us don't know enough theology to assent to all those beliefs. But these beliefs aren't necessary for salvation, and they certainly don't result in salvation.

The devil presumably believes everything that the Bible says and believes all the church creedal statements—unless there is something that we've got wrong! The devil believes them because he knows the truth better than we can—until we get to heaven. He even believes that Jesus can save sinners by the power of his victory on the cross—he knows about this because he was the one who was defeated. What the devil *doesn't* do is trust Jesus to save him!

FAITH IN AN ABILITY OR INSTITUTION

Faith is a foundation of the modern world, because it is needed by anyone who uses money. On every UK banknote it says "I promise to pay the bearer ..." This used to mean you could theoretically demand its value in gold at a bank counter. Now, according to an official response by the Bank of England, "public faith in the pound is maintained in a different way—through the Bank's operation of monetary policy."[1] Whether or not we have a strong faith in national banks, we all exhibit some faith when we accept these pretty pieces of paper or plastic in return for

---

1. See Bank of England, "What Is the Value of the Sterling Currency?" (TinyURL.com/PayBanknote).

our labor. We need even more faith in the monetary system if our wages turn up as a number in our online bank account. We, in turn, demand faith from others when we swap this otherwise worthless piece of paper for a cup of coffee or a taxi ride.

Our idea of faith has changed a lot since the time of the Bible. Athletes are encouraged to have faith in their abilities to win a race. They work hard at visualizing themselves running well and crossing the line first. If their conviction is strong enough, their mental resolve helps them run harder, so the depth and strength of their faith can help them to win. Most of us don't have the mental discipline for that kind of faith, but in any case, it isn't what the Bible meant.

The whole world relies on and revolves around faith. But it doesn't save people, because it isn't faith that saves. The important factor is who or what that faith lies in. Faith in the monetary system or faith in yourself may get you through life, but only faith in God will get you beyond this life.

TRUST IN A PERSON

The great rediscovery of Martin Luther and John Calvin in the sixteenth century was that our salvation is only possible because of a gift of God: "For it is by grace you have been saved, through faith—and this is not from yourselves, it is the gift of God" (Eph 2:8). We aren't saved by any good we do, or by asserting a particular belief system, or even by our faith in God's ability to save us. We are saved simply by God.

So what is the "gift" in Ephesians 2:8? Calvin said it is "salvation": "salvation is of grace ... 'it is the gift of God' ... and is received by faith alone, without the merit of works."[2] But some

---

2. John Calvin, *Commentary on Galatians and Ephesians*, CCEL (TinyURL.com/CalvinEph2-8).

Calvinists (later interpreters of Calvin) said that the gift is faith itself, because faith in God is too hard for a fallen human. As we saw at the beginning of this chapter, this was the way that the Peanuts character Linus thought about faith, as if you need to generate enough faith to be saved—except, unlike Linus, nobody is capable of generating this faith. However, if the gift is God's salvation, we simply have to trust God and receive the gift.

No Bible text says that salvation comes by belief in certain theological statements, by faith in our own ability, or even by our faith in the ability of God. We are not saved by *our* faith at all, but by God—so we trust he'll save us. All we need is the merest trust/faith/belief that *he* will save us. We need to accept God's offer and trust him.

FAITHFULNESS

Just when everything appears to be straightforward, James undermines this by understanding faith in a slightly different way. As we saw above, he was openly critical of those who claimed they were saved by "faith" alone. He realized that some people had misunderstood what this "faith" meant. His own understanding of the Greek word *pistis* was influenced by its use in the Greek translation of the Old Testament, where it translates the Hebrew word *amen*, meaning "true" or "faithful." For example, "the workers labored *faithfully*" and "great is your *faithfulness*" (2 Chr 34:12; Lam 3:23).

James realized that some people thought they didn't need to try and live righteous lives because they had misunderstood Paul's teaching about being saved by faith. They thought that faith by itself saved them. To correct them he explained, "Faith by itself, if it is not accompanied by action, is dead. ... I will show you my faith by my deeds" (Jas 2:17-18), that is, the proof of faith is in the doing. So if James were translating *pistis* into English, he'd use the word "faithful"—that is, letting faith change you so you are living "faithful" to God.

Actually, recent scholarship has found that Paul likewise sometimes used *pistis* to mean "faithfulness," though with a slightly different meaning. Paul referred to "the faithfulness of Jesus," but this hadn't been noticed before because the phrase was usually translated as "faith in Jesus" (Rom 3:21–22; Gal 2:16; 3:22–23; Phil 3:8–9). I think it's likely that this new interpretation is genuine Pauline theology that had been lost: that Jesus remained faithful throughout his life and especially during his tortured death. Paul was pointing out that the faithfulness of Jesus has saved us, because he was unwavering to the end, despite his suffering, which he could have avoided. So here too, the emphasis is not on being saved by our own faith, because Paul is highlighting that we are saved by Jesus.

The word *pistis* may not be straightforward to translate, but the concept of salvation by faith is simple. All that God requires is our trust. *Faith* in God and *belief* in God are merely other ways of saying that we *trust* him to save us. God wants to save sinners, and if they trust him to save them, he will. Of course, those who trust God will want to try to do his will and grow closer to him— so this trust leads to a whole lot more. But when you pick apart the details, in the end it all comes down to simple trust.

So is it correct to say that "we are saved by faith"? Yes! But it is not a Linus-style faith based on the strength of our convictions; we are saved by faith solely and simply because we are *saved by God*, whom we trust.

28

▼

Core Beliefs

What do we need to believe to be saved? There are very few essential doctrines and the list is surprisingly tricky to find in the Bible. But what if you don't have a Bible to read, so you don't know any of them?

After one exam at university, we were told that anyone with less than 0 percent had to see the professor. Fortunately I had 3 percent, though of course I didn't pass. The low marks occurred because of a strange examination technique that my medical school was experimenting with. They wanted to teach us that acting on the wrong answer can sometimes be worse than doing nothing at all, so wrong answers got negative marks. Those with less than zero had probably killed the patient!

There aren't many times when believing something to be true is a life-or-death situation, but becoming a Christian could be described that way. Although you don't become a Christian by simply believing a set of statements, it does nevertheless depend on a certain minimum set of beliefs. After all, if you are going to have faith in God, you have to believe he exists! What are the core beliefs—those that anyone needs to believe in order to be saved?

Seeing as this is so important, we might expect there to be a straightforward statement in the Bible about which beliefs are necessary—but there isn't. Nevertheless, you'd expect Christian leaders to know what they are, with a fairly unanimous

consensus. A quick trawl on the internet finds several sites list-
ing the doctrines you "have to" believe, but these collections are
bewilderingly different. My favorite among those that I found is
based on the acronym DOCTRINE: Deity of Christ, Original sinfulness, Canon of the Bible, Trinity, Resurrection, Incarnation,
New creation, and Eschatology (or "End times").[1]

A LOT TO LEARN

Some sites expect you to know a great many doctrines. One popular site has "99 Essential Doctrines," which they offer to teach
you during a three-year course.[2] Of course they don't say that
you have to know them all before becoming a Christian. However, in previous generations this might have been expected.
The established churches each had their own "shorter" cate-
chisms, which were the basis of questions you might be asked
before being baptized or confirmed. I rather like the Westmin-
ster Shorter Catechism's first question and answer: "Question:
What is the chief end of man? Answer: Man's chief end is to glorify God, and to enjoy him forever." However, when you realize
that this is the first of more than a hundred other questions you
have to memorize, it rather dulls the enjoyment.[3]

Anglicans have far fewer questions, though often the language is difficult. For example, "Question: What meanest thou
by this word Sacrament? Answer: I mean an outward and visible
sign of an inward and spiritual grace given unto us, ordained by
Christ himself, as a means whereby we receive the same, and a

---

1. Hank Hanegraaff, "What Is Essential Christian Doctrine?" (TinyURL.com/
EssentialDOC).

2. Ed Stetzer, "99 Essential Doctrines Christians Should Know" (TinyURL.
com/99Doctrines).

3. Example: TinyURL.com/PresCatechism.

pledge to assure us thereof."[4] Catholics have the most daunting task—a catechism consisting of 2,865 items.[5] There is a "simplified" version, though it is still very long,[6] and there is a brief version with "2,893 short and clear questions and answers," for example: "Question 2786: When is filial trust put to the test? Answer. Filial trust is put to the test in tribulations, when prayer seems not to be heard."[7]

Fortunately there is nothing like this in the Bible, except perhaps the short list of "elementary doctrines" at the start of Hebrews 6. These consist of repentance, faith in God, baptisms (or "cleansing rites"), laying on of hands, resurrection, and judgment. This is only partly helpful, because some of the meaning is lost in history—we can't be sure what the baptisms (plural) refer to, and laying on of hands may refer to receiving the Holy Spirit (Acts 8:17; 19:6), or healing (Acts 28:8), or ordination (1 Tim 5:22). Other places we might look for essential doctrines are the earliest summary of the faith that Paul says he "received" (1 Cor 11:23–26; 15:3–7). These teach about communion, Jesus' Scripture-fulfilling death, and the various resurrection appearances.

BIBLE BASICS

I think the best place to find out what a non-Christian needs to know is in the sermons preached to them in Acts. It looks like these are meant as a guide for other preachers, though Luke, the author, hasn't made it as easy as he might. Instead of repeating the same basic sermon several times throughout Acts, he divides it up, so we have to stitch it back together again from various

---

4. TinyURL.com/CatechismAnglicans.
5. TinyURL.com/CatechismCatholic.
6. TinyURL.com/ShorterCatholic.
7. TinyURL.com/FullCatholic.

places. Acts contains almost twenty sermons or speeches, but three of them are specifically highlighted as ones that contain the message of how to be saved.

The very first sermon, which grew the church from 120 people to more than 3,000, was preached at Pentecost. The listeners were all Jews, which may explain why it contains long expositions of the Old Testament. It was the crowd itself who brought Peter to the important point by asking: "What shall we do?" Peter gave a commendably succinct answer: "Repent and be baptized, every one of you, in the name of Jesus Christ for the forgiveness of your sins. And you will receive the gift of the Holy Spirit" (Acts 2:38). Paul is asked virtually the same question by his ex-jailer: "What must I do to be saved?" (Acts 16:30). He gave a commendably brief answer: "Believe in the Lord Jesus … you and your household." We are then told that he and all his household were baptized (16:31, 33).

Together, these give us the pair "repent and believe," which was a core religious response that all Jews would recognize and was also the same as the summary of preaching by John the Baptist (Mark 1:15; Acts 19:4). Jews wouldn't have been too surprised by "baptism," because the first immersion of a Gentile converting to Judaism was recognized as very important. So the most surprising thing for these converts is the emphasis on Jesus, whom they were to believe in and in whose name they were to be baptized.

Peter's sermon to Cornelius supplies the last bit of this basic message of salvation. The sermon is later described as "a message through which you and all your household will be saved" (Acts 11:14). In it, Peter explains the basics that they need to know about Jesus: Jesus is the Christ (i.e., the expected Messiah), Lord of all, anointed with the Holy Spirit by God, did miracles, was killed, then raised by God, and he will judge humanity, though by trusting him we can be forgiven all repented sins (Acts 10:36–46). I like the detail that "while Peter was still speaking these words, the Holy Spirit came on all who heard the message" (10:44). It is as if God couldn't wait any longer—he was longing to accept them into the kingdom. As soon as they'd heard the minimum necessary beliefs and understood them, they were in.

THE BOTTOM LINE

So, here, at last, are the core beliefs necessary for salvation. They are: the Trinity (Jesus is "Lord of all" and he is named with God and the Spirit together in 10:38), Jesus' death and resurrection, sin and judgment, and forgiveness by faith in Jesus. At first this looks like a random sample of basic doctrines, but actually they are all necessary for anyone who is going to repent and be baptized. Before you can repent, you need to know about sin, judgment, and the hope of forgiveness. And before you trust Jesus and get baptized in his name, you need to know why he is special.

There is one fact that the New Testament is particularly insistent that we believe: that Jesus is the Son of God. John says anyone who doesn't believe this isn't saved (John 3:18), and anyone who denies it is anti-Christian (1 John 2:22; 2 John 7). The reason for this emphasis is presumably that this was so difficult for Jews to accept. They had suffered terrible persecution for defending monotheism, and they regarded it as a denial of that doctrine.

The problem of Jesus' deity was debated and argued over for the next three centuries, until everyone agreed to the wording of a creed at the First Council of Nicaea (325). The Nicene Creed used in most churches today is actually from the First Council of Constantinople (381), because the original Council of Nicaea really only dealt with Jesus' deity. So the First Council of

Constantinople merged it with the Apostles' Creed, which presumably predated them both.

Although these creeds are relatively short, they aren't intended to define the knowledge necessary for salvation. After all, why would someone be barred from heaven for not knowing that that Jesus "suffered under Pontius Pilate"? They are the agreed statements issued at the end of a church conference to correct versions of the various beliefs that have been discussed. The conference of Nicaea discussed the Trinity, so the creed contains an agreed statement on this topic, but it doesn't mention anything about baptism or eternal life. Even when this creed was expanded by the Council of Constantinople it still didn't include Jesus' conception or his descent to hell. The older Apostles' Creed (which does have these two doctrines) is the fullest, but it doesn't mention anything about baptism or that God the Father "begot" Jesus—something the short Nicene creed mentions three times. So although they define a heretic (i.e., someone who disagrees with them), they do not define a believer.

THE CREEDS

The Nicene Creed (325) was expanded in 381 at the Council of Constantinople using largely the words of the Apostles' Creed. These creeds are so similar that they can be superimposed:

- Nicene Creed in **bold**

- Apostles' Creed in *italics*, with overlaps in ***bold italics***

- Constantinople revision of the Nicene Creed, which includes everything except the words in [square brackets]. These are only found in the Apostles' Creed.

We believe in one God, the Father Almighty,

Maker of heaven and earth, and of **all things visible and invisible.**

And in one Lord Jesus Christ, **the** *only-***begotten** *Son of God,* **begotten of the Father** before all worlds, **Light of Light, very God of very God, begotten, not made,**

being of one substance with the Father;

by whom all things were made;

who for us men, and for our salvation, came down from heaven, and was incarnate

[who was conceived] by the Holy Ghost and of the Virgin Mary, **and was made man;**

he was crucified for us under Pontius Pilate, and **suffered,** *and was buried, [he descended to the dead.]*

and the third day he rose again, according to the Scriptures,

and ascended into heaven, *and sitteth on the right hand of the Father;*

from thence he shall come again, with glory, **to judge the quick and the dead,** whose kingdom shall have no end.

And in the Holy Ghost, the Lord and Giver of life,

who proceedeth from the Father, who with the Father and the Son together is worshiped and glorified, who spake by the prophets.

[the communion of saints,] In one holy catholic and apostolic *Church;*

we acknowledge one baptism for *the remission of sins;*

we look for *the resurrection of the dead, and the life of the world to come.*

LIKE CORNELIUS

When we start asking how much ignorance will exclude us from heaven, we face the most difficult question: What about those who never hear about Jesus? I envy Abraham, who was able to bargain with God about saving lives in Sodom. Like him, I'd like to ask questions of God: "But what if someone believes in the love and holiness of God, but doesn't know about Jesus?" Or, "What if they love what they know about Jesus, but don't realize he is God?" And also like Abraham, I'd want to repeat the question he asked: "Will not the Judge of all the earth do right?" (Gen 18:25).

We shouldn't expect to find any answer to this question in the Bible. After all, it is written for people who are able to read it, so why should it tell us about those who *can't* read it? Its purpose is to address those who *can* read it—who *are* reading it! However, there are a couple of clues, and one of them occurs alongside the third salvation message in Acts.

Cornelius, who requested this message from Peter, was one of the many Romans who had found something genuine in the Jewish religion and attended synagogues to discover more. To explain why he'd called for Peter to come, he said: "I was in my house praying at this hour, at three in the afternoon. Suddenly a man in shining clothes stood before me and said, 'Cornelius, God has heard your prayer and remembered your gifts to the poor. Send to Joppa for Simon who is called Peter'" (Acts 10:30–32). The detail that jumps out to me is that God listens to the prayers of those who aren't Christians.

Because we are so familiar with the fact that access to God is through Jesus, we can easily forget that people in the Old Testament were able to pray and be heard. Cornelius was a pre-Christian believer, until the Holy Spirit fell on him, and this story shows that this category of people still continued to exist after

Jesus' death. God still listens to the prayers of those who don't know (or understand) about Jesus.

HOW TO PLEASE GOD

The second insight into pre-Christian believers comes in Hebrews, when it defines faith. It has a long chapter about people with faith (all before the New Testament, of course), and it starts by stating the minimum number of things we have to believe. There are only two! They are (1) that God exists and (2) that "he rewards those who earnestly seek him." This is so startling that it is worth reading over again: "Without faith it is impossible to please God, because anyone who comes to him must believe that he exists and that he rewards those who earnestly seek him" (Heb 11:6).

This isn't telling us how someone will be saved and receive the Holy Spirit—it is merely the pre-Christian or Old Testament faith. However, we shouldn't look down on it, because someone with this faith can "please God"—which is quite an amazing thing to aspire to!

These two items of faith are so minimal that they are worth our close consideration. To believe that "he exists" is a major matter today, when atheism is so popular, and many would regard it as an intelligent conclusion. But when this was written, there were extremely few atheists, if any. Even philosophers who thought that the universe ran without the action of any gods still believed they existed. So the fact that this is mentioned is impressive; it implies that the author really wants to give a full statement of what is required. The other item of faith, that "he rewards those who earnestly seek him," implies something like a judgment or reckoning as well as an effort expended to "seek him."

This doesn't describe those "good" people who think they deserve heaven because they believe they aren't as bad as others they could mention. Hebrews describes people who are seeking God, and they are presumably all too aware of their shortcomings. This means you can be sure that as soon as they realize Jesus was sent by God, they will become a Christian. They are as ready for Jesus as Cornelius was.

This little nugget of Scripture implies that God is still accepting people in an Old Testament way. However, we can't conclude too much from it because, as I said above, we shouldn't expect to find anything about such individuals in the Bible: if you have a Bible, you aren't going to be in this category. So we are left with questions we can't answer, such as: When or how are their sins forgiven? At a guess, I'd say they are like the Old Testament believers, who all benefit from the death of Christ, but not during their lifetime. Perhaps it happens soon after they die, or perhaps on their deathbed, when the barrier between heaven and earth is thinnest. We simply don't know.

These believers are missing out, as they themselves would agree when they learn the full truth. They would long to find Jesus and be filled with his Holy Spirit in this life. However, they are not despised or refused by God—Hebrews says that with their minimal faith and their seeking for him, they "please God." That is a considerable achievement, and if I can achieve even that accolade in this life, I'll be well satisfied.

▼

Conclusions

The three sections of this book have forced me to consider which doctrines are important, which are divisive, and which are so confusing that it is possible we have misunderstood the Bible.

O ne surprising realization I had while writing this book was how little it takes to "please" God. This is not a new discovery but is found in the Bible itself: we need merely to "believe that he exists and that he rewards those who seek him" (Heb 11:6). It was confirmed by drilling down in section 3 to the minimum list of doctrines necessary for salvation in the New Testament: Jesus' death, resurrection, and divinity, with an understanding that sin is followed by either judgment or by forgiveness if we repent and trust Jesus.

BOTH SIMPLE AND COMPLEX

Although this shows that the gospel is simple to grasp, looking at the details through first-century eyes also reminds us about the complexities that have kept theologians working for two thousand years. Concepts such as "Trinity" and "faith" are multifaceted in a way that translations can obscure. But the most complex topic in the New Testament turns out to be the means by which salvation comes through Jesus. This can't be portrayed by any single picture, so the writers use multiple images: redemption from slavery, a sacrifice of supreme value, vicarious suffering of sin's consequences, salvation obtained through mercy and grace, free forgiveness that necessitates repentance and obedience, and all this resulting in new birth or new creation, which can also be described like the adoption of a teenager.

Over time, as the church has merged these different representations of salvation, some have become obscured or conflated. For example, in this book we have found that the concept of suffering in the first century was entirely separate from the topic of sacrifice, so we tend to merge them—which means that we neglect the message of God's sacrificial generosity. Other topics are neglected in the Bible text because, paradoxically, although they are very important, they were so accepted or taken for granted that there was little need to mention them. Just as the Bible rarely teaches that God exists (because everyone already believed this), the topic of repentance was so overwhelmingly important and obvious in the first century that it isn't often mentioned. However, when we reinsert repentance into the background of beliefs, concepts such as sin and the need for forgiveness become self-evident.

CLEARER IN THE FIRST CENTURY

We have also found that other doctrines have become clearer when seen through the insights of first-century believers. The "unforgivable sin" has turned out to be something Jesus' contemporaries already knew about, so his teaching on this subject was actually something revolutionary about the nature of God. By contrast, original sin was an entirely novel teaching that isn't in the Bible, so we tend to confuse it with original sinfulness, which clearly is there. Unfathomable concepts such as faith and how prayer works are less confusing when seen through ancient eyes, though they are still mysterious.

Paradoxes such as predestination versus free will, or God's omnipotence versus human suffering, can be seen in a much clearer light when two thousand years of theological complexity are removed. Ultimately, of course, they aren't solved, because the Bible doesn't contain the solution—otherwise theologians wouldn't have had to work so hard. Nevertheless, uncovering the foundations of these issues has been illuminating.

The way we interpret and sometimes ignore texts is usually the weakest link in our doctrinal foundations—as we saw in the chapter on prooftexts. Occasionally the most likely reason is that the church has taken a wrong turn based on a misunderstanding. The New Testament is virtually silent on the issue of remarriage, for example, but the early church needed a clear message. Unfortunately, it came to profound conclusions on flimsy evidence. On the matter of eternal suffering in hell, however, the historic church didn't lack data in the Bible, but it seems that it chose to ignore part of the message found in many of the Bible texts on the subject. Our detailed look at the Bible text has helped us retrace some of those wrong turns.

TOWARD LESS DIVISION

I recently came across a disturbing Sunni Islamic doctrine called *firqa annajaat*, "the successful faction," which says that anyone from a rival denomination in Islam is destined for hellfire. Sunni Muslims, like Protestants, are divided into multiple denominations, and each one has inherited this doctrine. If they take it seriously, it means that anyone who doesn't believe *precisely* what their own denomination teaches will go to hell. I found this particularly disturbing because a similar belief is implicit among some Christians.

Divisions have been with us since the early chapters of Acts. Profound differences in what Christians believe about doctrines from birth and baptism through to the second advent have created many modern church splits. We disagree on whether to govern the church from the top down or bottom up, whether inspiration lies in the message of the Bible or its precise wording, and even whether we choose to follow God or are chosen by him.

Revisiting the biblical foundations for these differences won't solve them, but it does help us understand why other believers have come to different conclusions. We live in a complex universe, and God has not chosen to explain everything to us, so we should not automatically reject alternate conclusions based on the same revelation from God.

Some of our divisions are unavoidable because, for example, the same organization can't make decisions both by voting on each issue and also by following a single leader. But many *are* avoidable if we simply admit that the Bible doesn't make everything clear. We can't be certain of all the details implied by prophecy, and we can't hope to solve all theological paradoxes this side of eternity. Going back to the Bible with a little humility could heal many rifts and thereby fulfill Jesus' prayer to his Father "that they may be one as we are one" (John 17:11).

Doctrines are helpful summaries of what the Bible says, but we've seen that when they go beyond what the text says, they have the potential to confuse and divide. I see no harm in making conjectures about things the Bible doesn't state clearly, so long as we don't treat these ideas as dogma. We have also found that reading the text through the eyes of its original recipients can open our eyes to what it means. There is no harm in exploring God's word freely—especially in those areas that have been dismissed as "paradoxes" or other issues that are clearly problematic—as long as we come to the text in prayer and present our findings with humility. There is still much to discover!

Index

ANCIENT LITERATURE

BIBLE

SUBJECTS